Book of the American Civil War

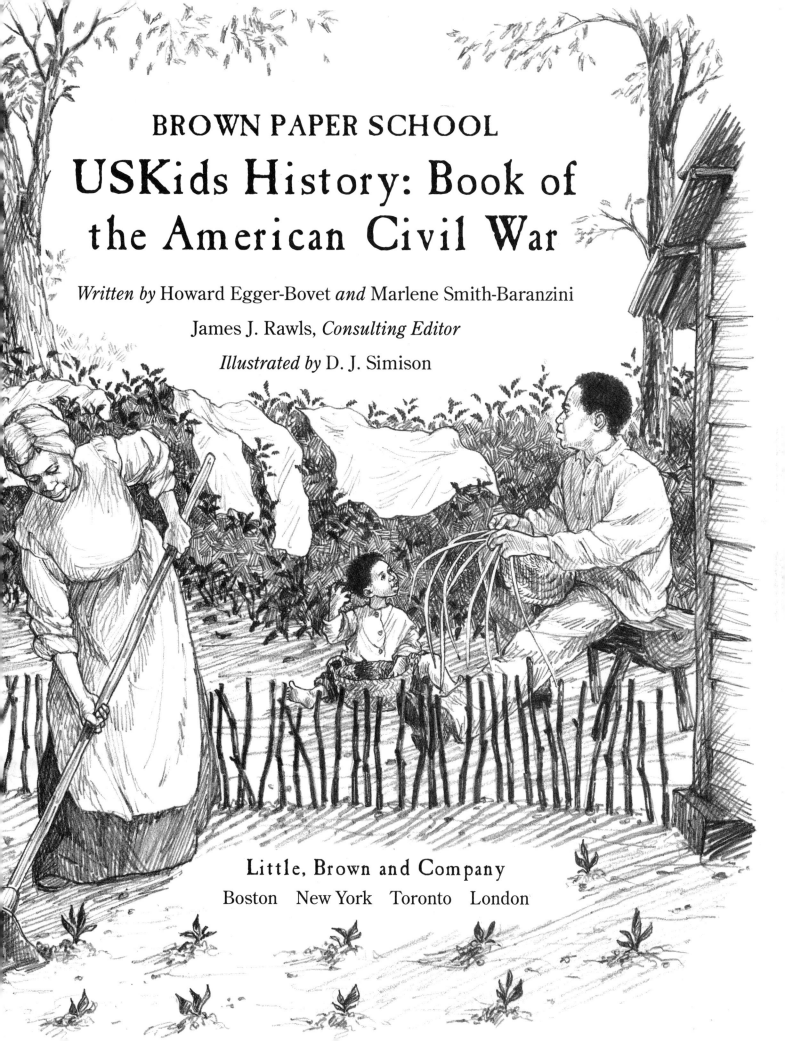

BROWN PAPER SCHOOL
USKids History: Book of the American Civil War

Written by Howard Egger-Bovet *and* Marlene Smith-Baranzini

James J. Rawls, *Consulting Editor*

Illustrated by D. J. Simison

Little, Brown and Company
Boston   New York   Toronto   London

A Yolla Bolly Press Book

Brown Paper School USKids History: Book of the American Civil War was edited and prepared for publication at The Yolla Bolly Press, Covelo, California. The series is under the supervision of James Robertson and Carolyn Robertson. Composition by Wilsted & Taylor Publishing Services, Oakland, California.

FIRST EDITION

MV-NY

Published simultaneously in Canada by Little, Brown & Company (Canada) Limited

Printed in the United States of America

Library of Congress Cataloging-in-Publication Data

Egger-Bovet, Howard.
   USKids history. Book of the American Civil War / written by Howard Egger-Bovet and Marlene Smith-Baranzini ; illustrated by D. J. Simison ; James J. Rawls, consulting editor.
      p.   cm. — (Brown paper school)
   "A Yolla Bolly Press book"
   Includes index.
   Summary: Focuses on the experiences of individuals in the Civil War through first-person narratives, from the perspective of both the North and the South, and speeches delivered before and during the conflict.
   ISBN 0-316-22239-9 (hardcover). — ISBN 0-316-22324-7 (pbk.)
   1. United States — History — Civil War, 1861–1865 — Personal narratives — Juvenile literature.   2. United States — History — Civil War, 1861–1865 — Sources — Juvenile literature. [1. United States — History — Civil War, 1861–1865 — Personal narratives.   2. United States — History — Civil War, 1861–1865 — Sources.]   I. Smith-Baranzini, Marlene.   II. Simison, D. J., ill.   III. Rawls, James J. IV. Title.   V. Series.
E464.E38   1998
973.7'8 — dc21   98-12849

Contents

Note: Activities and games are italicized.

Boys in Battle

On the cover of this book is a picture of a boy who risked his life in battle to rescue the flag of his country. He was awarded a medal for his bravery. His name was Nathaniel Gwynne, and you will find his story on page 77. Many boys and young men fought and many died in the Civil War. Some who died had only just arrived in America.

In 1858 Patrick, James, and their mother left Galway, Ireland, on a ship bound for New York. Their mother hoped America would offer her boys a better life.

She would never find out. During the journey she became ill and died. When the ship arrived in New York, Patrick and James were alone. They had no money to go back home.

Using their last dollars and their wits, James and Patrick found shelter and food. During the day they looked out for each other. At night they put themselves to sleep by singing a song their mother had taught them.

After several weeks, Patrick got a job in a factory. He asked the owner to hire his brother as well. James and Patrick worked long hours for little pay. James hated factory work. He wanted to find an outdoor job in the South. Patrick thought James's plan was too risky. They had jobs. They had a place to live, and they were making friends. Why go somewhere else?

But James had made up his mind. That night the two brothers put aside their differences and sang their bedtime song one last time. The next day Patrick went to work. James started his journey south.

Several years later, in 1862, America was in turmoil. Americans in the northern states were fighting against those in the South. It was the Civil War. Patrick joined the Union army in the North. James joined the Confederate army in the South.

One summer morning a battle was about to begin. Union and Confederate soldiers marched through the Virginia woods toward each other. As they marched, both Union and Confederate musicians played a song.

The music echoed clearly over the field at the woods' edge. Patrick, in the Union regiment, and James, in the Confederate regiment, were stunned by what they heard. Both armies were playing the song the boys' mother had taught them.

Patrick and James called out to each other. But their voices were lost in the sound of gunfire. Hours later, when the battle was over, Patrick walked among the dead bodies. At the field's edge was a fallen tree. Nearby, Patrick saw a body. There lay his brother, James, in his Confederate uniform, faceup in the afternoon sun, his chest bloody where the bullet had struck him.

Patrick wept, thinking about all the bullets he had fired during the battle. One of those bullets could have killed his brother. Patrick would never know. He softly sang the song that he and James loved, one last time. Then he buried his brother.

The American Civil War was one of the most difficult periods in the entire history of the United States. It was a bloody war in which Americans argued and finally fought with each other. Families were divided, often with tragic results. Fathers fought against their own sons. Brothers sometimes fought each other. Old friends became enemies. What could possibly have caused such things?

In this book you will learn why the southern states decided to separate from the northern states and why the civil war that resulted was so bitterly fought. You will also learn how our young country expanded to the West and how the addition of new states complicated the argument between the North and the South. Along the way, you will find stories, games, and activities that will help you understand this important chapter in the history of the United States.

Sarah and Hetty Broke the Law

"Father," she said, "I could study with Thomas."

Sarah Grimké stood by the parlor window in her family's mansion in Charleston. She watched the sky grow dark as she waited for her brother. The evening breeze ruffled her corkscrew curls. She listened for hooves on the cobblestones. She needed her brother's help.

Sarah wanted to talk with Thomas before his Latin lesson began, but now his tutor entered the parlor and began visiting with her parents. Sarah turned from the window. Quickly, she went to the sofa and sat beside her father. Her young household slave, Hetty, handed Sarah's sampler to her. Sarah ignored it.

"Latin will help Thomas greatly in college," the tutor told Judge Grimké. "He will advance quickly in his law classes."

"I expect my son to become one of Charleston's finest lawyers," Sarah's father said. He smiled at his daughter. "And this is my bright little Sarah," he added. "If she were a boy, what a fine lawyer *she* would make!"

Sarah's eyes sparkled. "Father," she said, "I could study with Thomas. I already speak French, and Latin will be easy." She had inherited Judge Grimké's brown eyes, and now they pleaded with him. "Please say yes."

But her mother spoke first. "No, child," she said firmly, "Latin isn't for girls. And Thomas must not be disturbed as he studies."

To Sarah's surprise, her father agreed. "You're a wise little parrot," he said, "and Latin *is* easy. But your time would be wasted, Sarah. You need to learn more useful things." Like Thomas, Sarah wanted to study law.

She reminded her father, "You say I should speak up when you and Thomas discuss politics. I will never debate like him if I must always be sewing, singing, and painting. Thomas doesn't learn such things." She waited, but her parents said nothing. As she started to speak again, the front door flew open.

Thomas rushed in, tossing his hat and riding gloves to Hetty. He apologized for his tardiness. With a wink at his sister, he moved to the chair beside her. Judge Grimké rose. "You two should begin," he said, looking at the young men. "Use the back parlor, but leave my papers as they are. Thomas, Sarah would like to join you, but we have said no." Sarah expected her brother to argue. He was six years older than she, and her closest friend. They told each other their secrets.

"Dear Sarah," he said gently, "listen to Father. You don't need Latin. But tomorrow we'll finish your French story." His words stung Sarah. She hated rules about what people could or could not learn. She was annoyed with her brother and her parents. She would learn Latin in spite of them. It would be her secret.

Another Secret

Sarah had another secret that Thomas didn't know about. Only Hetty knew, and the little black girl dared not tell a soul, for fear of what would happen to her.

As Thomas and his tutor left the room, Mrs. Grimké spoke sharply. "Hetty," she said firmly, "after Sarah is dressed in her nightgown, brush her hair well. Lately you are careless about removing the tangles."

Fear shot into the dark child's eyes. She stole a worried glance at Sarah. Sarah rose and pretended to yawn, hoping her mother did not see the exchange.

"Good night, Mother and Father," Sarah said. Hetty followed her to the bedroom. Hetty laid out Sarah's nightgown. She stirred the coals in the fireplace and added two logs, making a small fire. With a click, Sarah locked the door. She opened a drawer. The spelling book was exactly where she had hidden it.

Sarah brought the book, and the two girls stretched out before the hearth. The flames cast an orange glow over them as they huddled near the light.

"Begin here, Hetty," she whispered, pointing to a sentence. Slowly, the child began to read.

The Secret Discovered

Mrs. Grimké started upstairs to bed. Halfway down the long hallway, she stopped. Maybe a whipping would teach that servant how to brush Sarah's hair. She reached for Sarah's doorknob. It would not turn. She jiggled the knob, refusing to believe the door was locked.

The noise startled the girls. "Quick, Hetty!" whispered Sarah. "Lie down on the floor! I'll climb into bed." She closed the book as they scrambled to their feet. Someone pounded on the door.

"Sarah! What is this? Open this door at once," Mrs. Grimké ordered. Sarah heard her father's deep voice in the hallway, too. She would be punished if she disobeyed her mother. She did not know what she should do. Still in her ruffled dress, she turned the key. Mrs. Grimké marched in, followed by Sarah's father. Their eyes swept the room, from the fireplace to the children to the book. The spelling book! Sarah's father knew at once what she was doing.

"Sarah!" he said sternly. "How dare you teach a slave child her letters. You know that reading and writing are forbidden among Negroes. What are you thinking?" Judge Grimké took the book from her hands. He looked at Hetty, who was shaking and sobbing.

"Sarah didn't mean to do wrong," Hetty said. "It was my idea. I begged her."

"Hetty!" Sarah scolded. "You mustn't lie to save me." She faced her father and spoke

The No Reading Law

Sarah's father knew what the law said about teaching slaves to read. Sarah and her sisters taught Bible stories to black children in Sunday school, and they knew the law, too. They could not teach the black children to read for themselves.

South Carolina, like many states, had passed the "no reading" law back when it was still a colony, in 1740. It said that "any person who shall teach a slave to write or to employ any slave as a scribe [secretary] in writing, shall forfeit [be fined] 100 pounds." In Sarah's time, 100 pounds meant the value of that weight in sterling silver—an expensive fine for breaking the law.

Everyone knew the law. But some white people taught their slaves to read anyway.

Years Later, Sarah Remembered

In 1819, when Sarah Grimké was twenty-seven years old, she began a diary. She described how slavery had troubled her even as a child. This is how she described teaching Hetty to read:

"I took an almost malicious satisfaction in teaching my little waiting-maid at night, when she was supposed to be occupied in combing and brushing my long locks. The light was put out, the keyhole screened, and flat on our stomachs, before the fire, with the spelling-book under our eyes, we defied the laws of South Carolina."

bravely. "It is wrong that our poor slaves cannot say their letters. In Sunday school they can only listen to the stories of the Bible. I want Hetty to read for herself all the wonderful things we know."

Mrs. Grimké was upset. "Your disobedience will bring trouble to this family. If people learn that the child of Charleston's most important judge is teaching slaves to read . . ." Her voice trailed off. How would she control her strong-willed daughter? "This explains your knotted hair, Sarah. A lesson must be learned tonight," she said. "Hetty will go to the workhouse."

"No, Mother!" Sarah cried, moving in front of Hetty, as though she might protect the black child. "She mustn't be whipped. Please, Father. Spare her. I am the one who should be punished."

Judge Grimké studied his daughter. She was a daring child. Again and again he had told his children why teaching the slaves to read was a crime. Educated slaves might get dangerous ideas. He admired Sarah's quick wit, but he could not tolerate this.

"Sarah," her father began, "I am taking the book away. This must never happen again. Go to bed now. Tomorrow we will decide how to end this matter." He knew that Sarah's mother would choose a harsher punishment for Hetty, but whipping the slave would hurt Sarah, too. He did not want that. Hetty would not be chained in the workhouse, nor would Sarah be punished. But he was troubled. As he said good night to her, he knew that Sarah's ideas of right and wrong would not be easily corrected.

Hetty fled to the basement, where her bed was the dirt floor. Later, Sarah lay beneath her quilt, watching the fire die to ashes. She could not sleep. Life is very cruel, she thought.

B

B IS FOR BONDAGE

The land was good for farming. Colonial farmers in the 1600s quickly learned this fact as they settled in colonies such as Virginia, Maryland, and North and South Carolina. Southern farmers grew tobacco, sugar, indigo, rice, and cotton for profit. The larger the farm, the greater the profit.

Short of workers, farmers bought African slaves from traders to work their plantations. The slave system increased the farmers' profit. Farmers didn't pay slaves. They forced them to work for just food and shelter.

By 1850, when cotton became the most profitable crop for southern farmers to grow, they continued a 200-year-old tradition of slave labor to work the fields. By then it was a way of life.

Above: Most slaves lived in an environment like the one shown in this photograph. Port Royal Island, South Carolina, 1862.
Below: The painting *View Along the East Battery, Charleston*, by S. Barnard, shows some details of everyday life in 1831.

Paint a Folk Portrait

In the 1800s, many artists didn't go to school to study drawing and painting. They taught themselves, through practice and copying other artists. This style of untrained art is called "primitive," or folk, meaning unschooled. It can be identified by its everyday subjects, simple, clean lines, and lack of perspective. Art collectors search for primitive paintings because of their simple, charming style, and their historic value as America's earliest art.

Even if you take art classes in school, you can still paint in the style of a folk artist. Get the supplies you need from an art or crafts store, and then sketch a friend or pose in front of a full-length mirror and make a simple drawing that will be your guide.

You Will Need:

A beginner's set of acrylic or poster paints; drawing paper; pencil; eraser; two or three medium-size flat and round brushes; a 15-by-22-inch canvas board; an easel or heavy prop to support it while you paint; a plate for mixing colors; and a bowl of water for thinning paint and rinsing brushes.

1. Protect your work surface with newspaper. Set up your canvas so it doesn't slip.

2. In pencil, make a practice drawing on paper of your subject or model, that is, the person whose portrait you will paint. (Study the drawings in this book for ideas about proportion and shape. A head is basically egg-shaped, and the upper body is a rectangle with arms added.) Make your sketch large enough to fill the paper without crowding the edges. Later, you can draw an outdoor scene in the background or paint it a solid color. When your drawing is done, copy it onto your canvas. (You will paint over the pencil lines.)

3. Mix the colors you need on the plate. Experiment with the primary colors—red, yellow, and blue—to make other colors. Begin painting by outlining your subject in gray or brown, lightened with white, using the pointed brush. For a folk art style, paint with sharp, clean lines and solid colors.

4. As you paint, if you want to change something, let the canvas dry and then paint over it. You can change it as often as you like, until it pleases you.

5. When the painting is done, sign and date it in the lower corner, just as professional artists do. Add a simple wood frame, and hang it on the wall.

GIRLS, BOYS, AND ARTISTS

In families like Sarah's, daughters learned to keep house and to entertain their families and guests. They studied music, dancing, and art. They often practiced painting by copying artworks their families owned.

Sarah was born after the American Revolution, when the colonies won freedom from England. After that war, Americans wanted new styles and ideas that were "American." They wanted portraits of themselves and paintings that captured the American countryside. In children's portraits, exotic pets and toys showed that the family was wealthy.

Boys often did not study art, yet most artists in the nineteenth century were men. Charles Willson Peale, for example, was a Maryland craftsman who studied in London. He painted more than 240 portraits of famous Americans.

Peale believed that anyone could learn to paint. He taught his children to paint, and some of them became fine artists. His seventeen-year-old son Rembrandt painted President Washington's portrait in 1795.

Seventeen Rattles for Klaus

A huge snake lay in the dirt.

Henriette Morgan raced out of the dark cabin, squinting in the morning sunshine. Her long skirt brushed the grass as she hurried toward the barn. The dogs followed eagerly, expecting adventure.

"Hennie," her sixteen-year-old brother shouted from the house. "Wait. I'll hitch up the wagon for you." Henriette looked at Wilhelm, leaning against the doorway, in no hurry to do anything. Thirteen-year-old Hennie, on the other hand, wanted the wagon hitched and loaded, so they could leave.

"I can manage," she called back. "Get yourself dressed now." She had helped her brother hitch the wagon many times. It couldn't be that hard to do it alone.

That morning, before Father had left on horseback to visit his patients, Henriette and Mother had mixed dough and baked six creamy kuchens. Next she had packed a basket with cheeses and sausage and shaken her little sisters awake. Then she swept and made the beds.

Henriette was excited about visiting the Osvolds today. They had arrived in central Missouri only a month ago, and the two German families were becoming friends. The Osvolds had come from Munster, where Henriette's grandparents lived. Klaus Osvold, their oldest son, was six months older than Wilhelm, and one daughter, Maria, was Henriette's age.

Henriette had promised to help Maria learn English, so they could go to school together in the fall. She hoped that Klaus would go, too. He was reserved but friendly around her. When Henriette found herself tongue-tied at his questions, he smiled. Today she vowed to be bolder.

Henriette reached the barn and swung the doors open. She secured them with two large rocks, left there for that purpose. Inside, she led the big workhorse from its stall out to the front of the barn. The dogs barked, disappearing into corners, chasing the

Immigrant families faced many difficulties, and any day might bring new experiences for both parents and children. This story, inspired by a letter from a young German woman in Missouri to her brother in the "old country," describes a challenge that was unique to America.

scents of rodents. She pushed the horse in front of the wagon and brought the heavy harness gear from its pegs on the wall.

Working carefully, she lifted the collar and slipped the harness down over the horse's head, then secured all the fittings. She wrapped the straps tightly around the wagon shafts and buckled them. Finally, she fitted the bridle over the horse's head. There, she thought, leading the horse and wagon from the barn, there's nothing difficult about this.

She started back to the cabin to change her dress. But something stopped her. A few feet in front of her, a huge snake lay in the dirt. She froze in her tracks. Her eyes fell on its wide, beaded tail. From that distance, she could not count the rattles, but even one was too many. As she watched, the rattlesnake raised its triangular head and its thick patterned body moved toward the house.

Henriette's heart pounded as she decided what to do. If she screamed, the snake might coil and strike. If the horse saw it, the horse would bolt recklessly. The girl backed toward the barn, away from danger. When she reached a safer place, she would yell to her brother.

Suddenly the dogs bounded from the barn, running up beside her. They quickly discovered the rattlesnake and began barking wildly. The rattler coiled in self-defense. Its rattles vibrated madly, with a dry, rapid sound. The dogs circled the serpent, leaping, barking, and backing away as its jaws spread wide, revealing its sharp, venomous fangs.

Henriette ran back to the barn and grabbed the two heavy rocks propped against the doors. The dogs' frantic barking had brought Wilhelm from the cabin. He spotted the rattler.

"Hennie! Stay back! I'll get my rifle and shoot it!" Wilhelm disappeared into the cabin. With a rock in each hand, Henriette approached the snake. It writhed back and forth, unable to get past the dogs. Henriette took aim at its head. The first rock flew, landing with a thud against the snake's skull. Her aim was good. The snake twisted in pain, trying to get away.

Henriette drew her breath and aimed the second rock, throwing it even harder than the first. The rattler's tail curled tightly and then dropped. Its body jerked and twitched, but Henriette knew that it was dying.

She had no idea how long her brother and mother had been standing beside her. Sweat trickled down her forehead, and she was still shaking as she walked toward the cabin.

"Seventeen rattles," Wilhelm said, counting. "I'll get my knife and cut them off. I bet Klaus would like to see your morning's work." Henriette couldn't laugh yet, but she knew she wouldn't be tongue-tied when they reached the Osvolds' cabin.

HEARTS FILLED WITH HOPE

Most immigrants to America in the nineteenth century came from Europe. In the 1820s they made the Atlantic crossing for about $30 a ticket. It was a long, tiring voyage in a crowded, smelly ship. Often, no one met them when they arrived in this strange new land. But people of all ages made the journey. With some belongings and a little money, they set out.

People immigrated for many reasons. The Irish fled a potato famine. In Germany new farmland was scarce, machines in new factories took jobs away from other people, and people feared war. But America was booming. Land was cheap and plentiful. There were railroads, canals, and ships to build, and northern factories *needed* workers.

In the 1800s the British were the largest group to come to America, followed by the Germans. Millions more came from Ireland, France, Norway, and Sweden. People of other nationalities also arrived, their hearts filled with hope that the new world would be a good home.

How did people in the rest of the world learn about the United States? Some heard stories from travelers. Others read books written by visitors who had been here.

Many Germans read a book by Gottfried Duden. He was a lawyer who went looking for a place where Germans like himself might settle. In 1824 he arrived in Missouri. He spent four years exploring the western states and the territory along the Missouri River. He thought America was a great country, and in 1829 he published a book describing his discoveries.

Duden's timing was excellent. In Germany, life was hard. Duden's book convinced thousands of Germans that Missouri offered good land for farms and that with hard work they could all make fortunes.

THE GERMANS GAVE US CHRISTMAS

Every year, many American children wait impatiently for December to arrive. Whether snowdrifts pile high at the windows or rainstorms wash the trees bare, it is the season when Christians celebrate the birth of Jesus. For children, it is also a festive time of hanging stockings, making gifts, and waiting for Santa.

It wasn't always this way. In 1650 a group of young men in Plymouth Colony were scolded by the governor because they would not do their work on Christmas Day. That afternoon, the Puritan governor found them again, playing stoole-ball in the street. He took away their sticks and sent them home to spend the day in prayer.

Other Christian immigrants celebrated the day more joyfully. Some honored Christmas quietly, by going to church and sharing a special meal. But the Germans, more than any other group, gave Americans our modern symbols of Christmas. As the Germans held fast to their ancient traditions, their way of "Christmas keeping" spread throughout the world. Here is one of many legends that describe how Christmas began in Germany long ago.

In the Middle Ages, Germans celebrated the feast day of Adam and Eve on December 24 by cutting down an evergreen tree. They hung apples on the tree, to represent the Garden of Eden and humanity's temptation to eat the forbidden fruit. A ring of lighted candles, symbolizing Christ as the Light of the World, surrounded the tree.

The early Germans blended their Christian worship with the pagan celebration of the winter solstice on December 21. It was customary for Thor, the Yule god, and Hertha, goddess of the home, to bring gifts to the people.

In later centuries, people placed the candles on the tree (a risky practice that has ended!), along with thin, round cookies that stood for the Host, or body of Christ. As the celebration grew, hand-blown red glass ornaments replaced the apples, and the tree became the symbol of everlasting life. From this beginning, Advent wreaths, nativity scenes, angels, tinsel, and Twelfth Night ceremonies added festivity to Christmas.

A IS FOR ANCESTORS

You are the youngest link in a family chain that began centuries ago. This chain of relatives you come from is called your ancestors. You are their descendant; that is, you have come down, or descended, from them. The record of family descendants is called genealogy (jee-nee-AHL-uh-jee). When people keep good records of births, marriages, and deaths, they can trace their genealogy a long way back. Birth, marriage, and death records, called vital statistics, are also recorded by counties, states, and the federal government. Ask your parents to show you your birth certificate, and make a copy of it. It is the official proof of your birth, and it is your first vital statistic.

Counting Newcomers

In 1820 the United States government began keeping records of immigrants. That year, more than 8,000 people arrived, making the total population nearly 10 million people.

Beginning in 1820, the immigrant population almost doubled every five years. By 1850 immigrants made up 15 percent of the total population. By 1860 nearly one in seven Americans had been born in a foreign country. One fourth of the population was German or part German.

In 1860 most Americans lived on farms in rural areas. The six largest cities with over 100,000 people were: Boston, Massachusetts; New York City and Brooklyn, New York; Baltimore, Maryland; Philadelphia, Pennsylvania; and Cincinnati, Ohio. San Francisco was the only city west of the Mississippi River with more than 35,000 people.

Bake a Fruit Kuchen

Immigrant women learned to cook with new foods they discovered in America. But their favorite foods from the "old country" were always the heart of family celebrations and holiday meals. As children grew up and had families of their own, cooking from Grandma's recipes anchored them to their ancestors and created new traditions. In this way, dishes from around the world passed from mother to daughter, cousin, and friend, and appeared on supper tables far from where they originated.

This old recipe for an easy German fruit kuchen, or cake (it's really much like a pie), has traveled thousands of miles since it was first served in Germany long ago. Surprise your family by serving it for brunch or dessert. It can be baked a day ahead and refrigerated until serving time.

(Makes one 9-inch pie)
For the crust:

12-oz. package of refrigerator biscuits

For the filling:

2 eggs

$1/2$ pint whipping cream

$1/2$ cup sugar

2 cups sliced fruit, such as peaches, bananas, apples, or canned berries

a dash of cinnamon or nutmeg

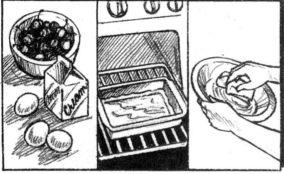

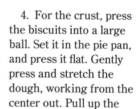

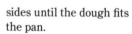

1. Preheat the oven to 400°.

2. With an eggbeater or whisk, mix the eggs, cream, and sugar together in a small bowl. Place the bowl inside a larger bowl, and carefully fill the larger bowl with hot water to warm the cream to room temperature while you prepare the crust.

3. Grease a 9-inch pie pan.

4. For the crust, press the biscuits into a large ball. Set it in the pie pan, and press it flat. Gently press and stretch the dough, working from the center out. Pull up the sides until the dough fits the pan.

5. Slice the fruit, and spread it over the dough.

6. When the cream mix is warm, pour it over the fruit. Sprinkle the top with

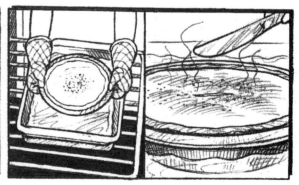

cinnamon or nutmeg, and carefully place it in the oven.

7. Lower the heat to 375°, and bake the kuchen for 15 minutes. Reduce the heat to 350°, and bake it for another 15 or 20 minutes, until the crust is golden and the filling is thick. (The center will thicken a little more as the kuchen cools.) Serve it warm or cold.

Dig Up Your Family's History

Unless you're a full-blooded American Indian, your family moved to this country from another place in the world. Maybe you were born here but your great-great-grandparents arrived from somewhere else. Or maybe your grandparents came from several countries. Where did they come from, and why did they come here?

Knowing your family's journey is important because it helps you know who *you* are. As you discover ancestors, you will find out how they contributed to history. Maybe they built cars or hospitals, or raised and sold crops. You may have inherited a trait from a relative you didn't know about.

Start digging up your own history by recording one or two generations of your family. Begin with your mother's or your father's side of the family. Your mother's people are called your *maternal* ancestors; your father's are *paternal* ancestors. For this activity, you will start with yourself and work backwards, listing as many ancestors as you can.

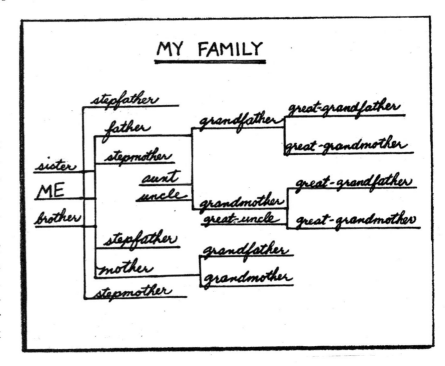

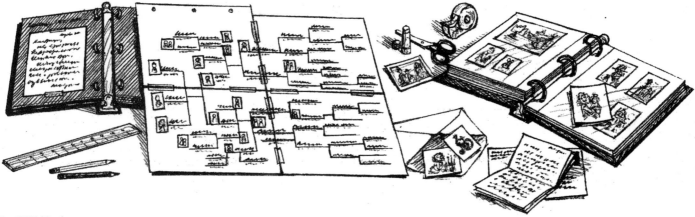

You Will Need:

A sturdy three-ring binder; unlined three-ring binder paper; pencils (one with red lead); a ruler; and a family photograph album.

1. Turn your paper sideways so it's wide. At the top, write *My Family Tree.* Put today's date on the paper. Whenever you add more information, add the new date.

2. Using a ruler, copy the diagram on this page. It provides spaces for four generations of family names. The pairs of lines that are connected are *marriage lines.* Add stepparent lines if you need them. The single line at the left is for your name.

3. Start with your generation. Write your name in red on the single line. Above or below your name (in order of the oldest first), draw extra lines for your brothers and sisters, and write their names in regular pencil. Add the year each child was born. If someone died, add that year.

4. Now do the second generation—your parents. In red, write their names on the first *pair* of lines to the right of yours. (Red indicates direct blood lines.) Fathers' names are usually written above mothers' names. Add their birth years. Add your mother's "maiden" (unmarried) surname if it's different from her married name. In pencil, add the names of your aunts and uncles as you did for your siblings.

5. Record names and birth and death years for as far back as your family can remember. See if your family photograph album has extra pictures—or make copies—that you can cut out and glue beside family names. Photocopy your family tree, and enclose it with a letter to your grandmother or other relatives who can add names and pictures.

6. You can enlarge your chart by redrawing it on larger paper or taping extra pages to the top or sides. Adding the names of cities or countries where relatives were born helps you see how your family has moved—or immigrated—from one place to another and what nationalities you share.

7. Add stories. Ask your relatives to write stories about their lives, or write what they tell you. Put their full name and date on the story, and keep it in your binder. Store your binder in a safe place. Your family tree will double if you marry when you grow up.

Henry and the Wooden Ruler

Something strange occurred at Concord Grammar School in September of 1837. In most ways, the first two weeks of lessons went by without a hitch. Oh, the girls noticed that the wooden benches were crowded now that the farm boys were back at school after a summer of working in the fields. And some people in town thought the new teacher, Mr. Henry David Thoreau (thor-OH), was a little unusual. But that was all right with them.

In the village of Concord, with its white wooden houses and about 2,000 people, everyone knew the Thoreaus. They were intelligent, honest, neighborly, and hardworking. The Thoreaus made and sold some of the finest lead pencils in America. Henry could be a little different if he wanted to. Not much was said after he graduated from Harvard College in August of 1837 and changed his name around, from David Henry to Henry David.

Nature fascinated Henry. The best place to explore it, he believed, was right around Concord. Other young adventurers from New England might pack their bags and explore faraway places like the Michigan territory or the wilderness beyond the Mississippi River. But Henry thought about the wonders of the earth closer to home.

In his idle hours, he went walking. He called it sauntering. He usually headed through the woods to the Concord River. Slow-moving and wide, the river flowed silently through the village. Wading along a shallow edge, Henry stopped to observe the ripples sparkling in the sunlight and to smell his favorite flower, the white water lily. He could spend hours beside the river, studying the plants, insects, and minnows.

Henry was making pencils in his father's workshop one day when he heard that the town grammar school needed a teacher. He decided to try for the job. He was a

In his idle hours, he went walking.

Henry David Thoreau lived a simple life. A few clothes, some hand tools, and pencils and notebooks were all he wanted. He lived with his friends, doing chores in exchange for rent. He grew his own vegetables and borrowed the books he wanted to read.

Every day Thoreau went out exploring nature. He liked to carry a slice of plum cake. This way, he said, he could eat his dinner and his dessert at the same time.

When people asked about his work, he sometimes said he was an inspector of snowstorms and rainstorms. Today we would call him a naturalist.

good tutor, and teaching paid well enough. But in the first days of school, the young schoolmaster surprised his class with an odd remark.

"I will not whip anyone with the willow switch," he announced. "Nor do I think it's right to swat your palms or knees with this ferrule," he added, tapping his wooden ruler.

More than one set of skeptical parents heard from their children about their teacher's strange way of keeping order. At supper tables, grown-ups argued about Thoreau's new teaching method. It had never been tried in American schools before, and of course it wouldn't work. People were so certain, in fact, that they sent a member of the school committee to watch Mr. Thoreau teach his students.

They chose Deacon Cyrus Stow. He was one of the men who had hired young Thoreau. One morning during the second week of school, Deacon Stow knocked on the heavy schoolhouse door. After greeting the teacher, he marched to the front of the classroom, where he could see everything.

Mr. Thoreau's inkwell and books were neatly arranged on his desk. Wearing his old green jacket and mended trousers, he stood on the platform a little above his students. The children sat on plain wooden benches.

At reading time, the sharp-nosed teacher with his gray-blue eyes called a row of students to stand before his desk. As they recited their lesson, Mr. Thoreau never raised the ruler or waved the switch. The deacon saw that the pupils were prepared and their answers were correct. But without whipping, how could the students learn discipline?

The deacon had seen enough. When he left, he called a meeting of the school com-

Henry's Father's Pencil

Henry Thoreau's father was one of the first pencil makers in the United States. Henry convinced his father to use imported Bavarian clay and graphite in their pencils. Soon the Thoreau pencil had the best, darkest "lead" of any pencil in America. Henry also invented a drill that could bore a hole in the wood case so the "lead" could be pushed into it. The Thoreau pencil won prizes for its quality and design.

In 1890 a company in Austria painted its pencils yellow, and the color soon stood for quality. The pencil did not have an eraser yet, though. Writers rubbed off their mistakes with a small lump of bread dough. In 1893 a rubber eraser was added to the pencil end.

mittee. He reported what he had seen in Henry's classroom. The committee agreed with him. If Thoreau would not use the switch, he would lose his position. They went to visit the new teacher.

A little uneasily, Henry stood before them.

"Mr. Thoreau," the deacon said firmly, "you will spoil the school if you do not use the ferrule and the whip when your students do not behave."

The young schoolteacher took a deep breath. He did not believe children learned better when they were whipped. They behaved when he reasoned with them. Would he allow the school board to tell him how to run his class? Should he go against his principles and punish his students just to satisfy the school committee?

Henry took a few days to make up his mind. Before September was over, the school committee returned to hear his decision. Henry gave them his answer. After school, he lined up six children he had chosen at random. Some were fine students, and others had been used to a swat now and then. To Henry, it made no difference who they were or what they had done. He knew that the school committee only wanted to see that he could punish. He would show them.

"Outside," he commanded the six students. Taking the ruler from his desk, he went down the row, one by one, striking each student in turn. When he finished, he turned to the deacon.

"There," he said, sounding irritated. "You have your ferruled students, if you think that will make them scholars. As for me, I do not. I submit my resignation, here and now."

With that, he dismissed the children. He put down the ruler, collected his books and his overcoat, and left.

"I have just ended my teaching career at Concord Grammar School," he realized. "What will I do now?" he wondered as he headed toward the river.

SPENDING TIME WITH INDIANS

For most Americans, a "good life" meant buying farmland and building a solid house. They didn't want to live naturally in the woods. They cleared trees, killed animals they considered dangerous, and planted crops. They took the land they wanted, even killing Indians to get it. Indians had no rights; they could not even vote as U.S. citizens until 1948.

Henry Thoreau believed Indians understood the natural, "wild" world. He believed they were masterful warriors. He built himself a small cabin at Walden Pond, to save money and so he could "live like an Indian."

In the 1850s he made two trips into Maine to explore and to study Indians. Each time, he hired an Indian guide. Joe Aitteon, a twenty-four-year-old Abenaki, and later Joe Polis, a Penobscot guide, took Henry up the Penobscot River to Moosehead Lake. Henry wrote about his friend Polis, but to protect the Indian's privacy, he would not publish his account. After his death, it became the book *Into the Maine Woods*.

SHOCKING SHORT SKIRTS

If you were a young woman in the late 1840s, your job would probably be taking care of your house and children. In the morning, you would dress in several layers of clothing. One of these, a tight corset, laced up like a shoe. It kept your back straight, pinched your waist as small as possible, squeezed your insides, and made natural breathing impossible. Your skirt touched the floor, with several petticoats underneath to make it stand out wide. The bottom was always dirty from floors and streets. Women tripped on their hems while carrying children or objects up stairs, or stumbled after bending down to pick something up.

In 1848 Elizabeth Smith Miller came home from a trip to Europe and sewed herself a new outfit like those she had seen in Switzerland. The top fit more loosely, and the full skirt came just below her knees. Under the skirt went a pair of baggy pants, gathered at the ankles and finished with a ruffle.

Mrs. Elizabeth Stanton watched with surprise as her cousin Elizabeth carried a baby and a lamp upstairs without tripping or tumbling. Mrs. Stanton wanted the new outfit, too. In a few weeks, the two women in their dresses and pants stopped at the post office on their way to a meeting. The deputy postmistress, Amelia Bloomer, saw the clothes and exclaimed about how practical they were. She wrote about them in a little newspaper she printed. Women began asking for patterns and sewing instructions. Amelia told everyone that Elizabeth Smith Miller had created the design, but people called them bloomers, after Mrs. Bloomer.

Many men and women alike were shocked to see women wearing pants in public. Some women even cried in shame when their friends wore them. But farm women, mill girls, and others decided that bloomers were a good idea. The bloomer costume lasted only a few years. Most of the women who wore it were in favor of changing more than their manner of dress. Many of them fought to get voting rights for women. In fact, the meeting that Elizabeth Miller and Elizabeth Stanton attended, dressed in their bloomers, was the first convention for women's rights. It was held in Seneca Falls, New York, in 1848. It wasn't until seventy-two years later, in 1920, that the Nineteenth Amendment to the U.S. Constitution finally granted female citizens of the United States the right to vote.

HAVE A SYLVESTER GRAHAM CRACKER

In the 1830s and '40s, many Americans believed they should try to improve life for those who were less fortunate. These reformers improved prison conditions, helped people who were mentally ill, and protected children against harmful working conditions. One way they spread their ideas was by giving lectures, which were also reported in newspapers.

Sylvester Graham, a vegetarian minister who lived in Connecticut, lectured on the importance of eating a healthful diet, taking cold showers, and sleeping on a firm mattress. Many Americans took his advice and followed the Graham diet. He taught people to bake bread using coarse flour they ground themselves.

People named this fibrous flour "graham" flour, after him. Now it's called whole wheat flour.

In 1829 Mr. Graham created a coarse wheat cracker that is still popular today. But he might shudder to see his simple Graham crackers on a camping trip today: filled with gooey marshmallows and melted chocolate bars!

New Ideas About Life

Thoreau, his best friend, Ralph Waldo Emerson, and their other friends in Concord liked to talk about ideas. Their favorite discussions centered on God, morals, nature, and intuition. They called themselves Transcendentalists.

They wrote essays that expressed their ideas. They were fine poets, too. Their poetry and philosophical writings attracted attention. The Transcendentalists, especially Thoreau and Emerson, became famous in America and much of the rest of the world.

Stones Didn't Frighten the Bride

Please Return the Socks

One of the most difficult things Mrs. Mary Grimké ever did was to give three of her five daughters permission to move north to Philadelphia. She listened to Sarah and Angelina argue that she should free her slaves. But then, she asked them, who would take care of her when she was old?

When Angelina and Theodore Weld married, Mrs. Grimké was happy. She wrote letters to her daughter more often. She sent neighborhood news and homemade pickles. She offered motherly advice to the couple.

She sent her new son-in-law, Theodore, three pairs of stockings. She told him that the stockings were made of cotton grown and picked by the slaves. If he was unwilling to wear them because of this, she would understand, and would appreciate it if he would return them to her.

Angelina took her place on the speaker's platform. In her plain Quaker bonnet and dark dress, her hair pulled back simply, she did not look like a woman who might cause trouble. But for the past year, Angelina Grimké Weld had been speaking in public, telling people why slavery was wrong. She and her older sister Sarah Grimké had dedicated their lives to helping slaves. They would not give up until all black Americans were free.

Angelina looked over the faces gathered in Pennsylvania Hall, Philadelphia's new center for public lectures. Anticipation filled the air. Before her were 3,000 women and a small number of men. They filled all the seats and lined the walls. Many more stood at the back of the hall. The women's anti-slavery convention was beginning.

Outside there was a crowd of protestors. Angry voices shouted, "Slaves are property! People have a right to their property, and they should be left alone with it!" Trouble was expected that night. Angelina had arrived early to avoid it.

When it was her turn to speak, Angelina rose. Facing the audience, she searched the crowd for her husband, handsome Theodore Weld, a popular leader in the national anti-slavery movement. The presence of Theodore and other men no longer made her nervous. They had begun coming to her lectures earlier this year, in Boston and New York. She saw her sister, sitting among the Quaker bonnets. Angelina was also glad to see that blacks had come. Her message was *about* them, about the evils of slavery. She wanted everyone to hear it.

Angelina Weld was an unusual woman, and the people in the hall listened intently as she spoke. The plain, slender woman was a Southerner. She told the audience about her life in Charleston, living with slaves. She could name black husbands who were not free to live with their wives and black children who were sold and taken away from their parents. She had seen slaves who were beaten until they couldn't walk. *They* were the reason she fought to end slavery.

Suddenly a window shattered and glass flew into the room. The angry crowd outside was hurling stones into the hall. The noise startled everyone, but Angelina was not afraid. The protestors, in fact, became the perfect example for her talk. She drew a breath and looked sharply at the audience.

"What is a mob?" she demanded. "What would the breaking of every window be? . . . What if that mob should now burst in upon us, breaking up our meeting and commit[ting] violence upon our persons? Would this be anything compared with what the slaves endure? No, no: and we do not remember them . . . if we shrink in time of peril." More stones shattered more glass. The crowd inside was restless and afraid. But Angelina waited. When everyone was calm, she continued. The protestors outside shouted loudly. She ignored the noise and went on.

For nearly an hour, the southern-born aristocrat, turned Quaker, told the gathering why slavery was wrong and how women—who could not yet vote—could help abolish it.

Angelina Grimké Weld finished speaking. Once again, her message had won an audience. As she sat down, the thunder of 3,000 pairs of clapping hands filled the air.

A FAMILY TORN

Sarah Grimké moved to Philadelphia from Charleston in 1821. She and her father had come north in 1819, because he needed medical treatment. Judge Grimké's doctor had told him that the Quaker doctors in Philadelphia were the best in America. While she was there, Sarah discovered freedom in the city. Women could go out alone. People walked everywhere—to the market or just for pleasure. The Quakers were friendly. And most of the black people were not slaves. They were freemen, who earned wages for their work.

In spite of the Quaker doctors, Judge Grimké grew worse. Sarah was with him when he died. She arranged for his burial and then went home to Charleston, alone. At once, she felt out of place.

To Sarah's family, black people were only property, and nothing she said could change their attitudes. Sarah spent many hours in prayer, asking for guidance. Finally, in 1821, her mother agreed that Sarah and her older sister Anna could move to Philadelphia.

Later, Sarah invited Angelina, her youngest sister, to come for a visit. When she arrived in Philadelphia, Angelina too saw many differences between northern and southern life. She liked Quaker ideas about women's rights and freedom for blacks.

After her visit, Angelina returned to Charleston eager to change her family's attitudes toward slavery. She couldn't, but she kept trying until her mother, her brothers, and even her sisters-in-law were angry with her. Even when they agreed that slavery might be wrong, they couldn't imagine living without it.

During this time, Angelina had an unusual experience. A voice within her told her she would do something important with her life. To Angelina, this was a message to fight against slavery. In 1829, with her mother's reluctant approval, she packed her possessions and left for Philadelphia.

THE FEMALE ANTI-SLAVERY SOCIETY

Women were not permitted to join anti-slavery societies begun by men, so they organized their own groups. They called their meetings literary circles or sewing societies. They sewed clothing or quilts they would secretly send to slaves, and they listened to abolitionist speakers, such as Sarah and Angelina Grimké, Lucretia Mott, Lucy Stone, and Elizabeth Blackwell. As more women joined these societies, they moved their meetings to churches or town halls.

Hundreds of women from northern states met in Philadelphia in May 1838 to attend the convention of the Female Anti-Slavery Society. For four days they held meetings, planned activities, and heard women leaders condemn slavery.

Breaking the tradition of excluding men from their meetings, they boldly asked William Lloyd Garrison to begin the first evening lecture. Garrison, a famous, fiery editor of an anti-slavery newspaper, introduced the evening's three women speakers. Men and blacks were also invited to hear the lecture in Pennsylvania Hall. This was the first time that Theodore Weld, a founder of the American Anti-Slavery Society, heard his new wife speak in public.

White Slaves

Many people thought the Grimké sisters should keep their noses out of issues like slavery. Angelina, quick with an answer to comments like this one, replied that if women did not act— because they had no *right* to act—then they should think of themselves as the "white slaves of the North."

Until 1920 American women could not vote. When a woman married, the law said her property became her husband's. Angelina and Sarah knew these laws needed to be changed. But the problem of slavery was more important than the restrictions on women's rights. When they spoke in public, they tried not to talk about women's rights. But *because* they were women, people couldn't ignore it. Women's rights began to creep into the movement to end slavery. Soon Sarah Grimké was writing only about women's rights, urging women to demand better pay for their work, the right to vote, and other rights that men enjoyed.

Make a Civil War Alphabet Book

Throughout this book, but not in any order, is a series of boxed alphabet letters. Each one introduces a word that explains something important about the Civil War, or about *you* and the war. Some letters are missing, so you can complete the alphabet by choosing words of your own.

Using the letters in this book as guides, trace or design your own set, one to a page. Use bright construction paper, poster paints, or colored markers to design the letters. Add the word to go with the letter, and write a simple explanation of the word or use the ones in this book.

You Will Need:

A three-ring binder or plastic presentation cover with three-hole fasteners; thirty or more sheets of drawing paper; scissors; glue; tape; poster paints; colored markers; and colored glue for designing alphabet letters, making pictures, and decorating your book's cover.

1. Design the letters of the alphabet, *A* to *Z*, drawing one large, ornate letter per page. Then for each letter, add a word and its meaning. You can use words and meanings found in this book or choose your own. Your alphabet book might feature Civil War weapons, or women and their war deeds, or names of famous military officers. (For the letter *B*, we chose *Bondage*, but *Black Powder* or *Bull Run* are good choices, too.) If the words express your interests, the book will become your personal history of the war.

B is for Black Powder.

2. When you have drawn all the letters and written all the words, put them in order—either alphabetically or with your favorite ones first. Add a blank page at the front, followed by a page for the book's title. If you have ancestors who fought in the war, or neighbors whose ancestors did, add their stories to the *A* page. Ask family members to write their thoughts or memories about the war. If you have them, paste photographs of your Civil War ancestors on this page, too, along with your own picture. (Add extra pages as you need them.)

T is for Tennessee, one of the Confederate states.

F IS FOR FREE BLACKS

By 1860 there were more than 4 million blacks in America, and almost half a million of them were free. They had become free in various ways. Many were born to free black parents. Others put aside money and bought their freedom, and some had masters who grew to oppose slavery and freed them. Still others ran away from their owners and were lucky—and clever—enough to live as free blacks without being discovered. Many free blacks changed their names, often dropping the last name their master had given them.

A is for Abraham Lincoln. He was the 16th President. He led the North during the Civil War.

3. When you visit battlefields or war monuments, collect postcards to add to your book. If you have old Civil War medals, uniform buttons, or paper documents, make a collage —a display of mixed materials—that includes them.

(Copy the documents, and preserve the originals in a safe place.)

4. What is the most interesting or important part of the war to you? After you have decided, make a drawing of it for the cover of your book.

Ask a copy shop to laminate it for protection. When your book is finished, keep it handy so you can add to it as you learn more about the war that almost destroyed the American nation.

PLAYING WITH SLAVES

In the book *The Children of Blandensfield,* Evelyn Ward, a white woman, remembers growing up on her family's farm in Blandensfield, Virginia, during the Civil War.

"I will begin with one September morning in 1860. . . . The woods were lovely at that hour. There was much to see. Now the fall was coming in, fresh and crisp. Wild hops were in bloom, goldenrod and asters were coming out. Not far from the spring there were two grapevine swings and, if we went early enough, we could get a swing all around, though there were so many of us. There were Stell, Evie, and Fonnie, the little white girls; Amy and Maria, our little black maids, and Lewis, the son of our dear nurse Louisa. . . .

"We children had our jobs, any number of them. There was the sage to be picked for the sausage, the golden crab apples to be gathered for jelly. . . . After frost came, chestnuts would be dropping freely. We would have to be out early every morning to pick them up before the hogs could get there. Our biggest job was to pick the cotton, but that would wait till November when the cotton bolls would open. Father always raised a small supply of cotton that was picked by the children of the place, black and white. . . .

"That afternoon we went down to gather the golden crabs [apples]. Lucy and Harry led. They were the nearest in age to us, the little girls. Jack, the fly-brush boy, was there too, and all the little fry, white and black. With such a crowd, we couldn't help but have a good time. . . .

"'I'll tell you what we'll do,' said Lucy as we walked back to the house with the apples. 'Let's make a whole set of new rag babies, and when we cross the ferry, let's play they are shipwrecked, and throw them into the river.'

"'Oh!' cried Fonnie in extreme agony. She loved the thought of all those new rag babies, and then to throw them into the river!

"Stell and Evie thought it a fine plan. As soon as they reached the house, they went up into the

nursery. It was growing dusk. Lucy got a candle. . . . She put it on a little table near by the chest that held scraps and doll-baby rags, and all of us dived in eagerly to pick out pretty pieces and bits to dress the dolls that were to be sacrificed. What a good time we had! Lucy was delightful. She made such beautiful rag dolls, and was so good to all of us. Harry was lovely, too. He could sew as if he were a girl. He often made things for our dolls.

"Now Lucy was busy making beautiful creatures, dressing them gorgeously, and they were all to be thrown into the river! Fonnie handled each one with woe in her face. Especially she loved a boy rag baby dressed in linen trousers, a black Norfolk jacket, and a black-velvet cap. His name was Edwin. Lucy named him that because she said she knew he was a sneak and a tell-tale who wouldn't own up to his own bad deeds, and that 'Edwin' was a goody-goody name that suited him. The more Edwin was abused, the more Fonnie loved him."

NO SLAVES HERE

Southern slave owners watched unhappily. In 1807 President Thomas Jefferson and Congress made it illegal for an American to bring slaves from Africa to America.

In 1820, because the North had more votes than the South, the Congress passed the Missouri Compromise. It was a way for the North to stop the spread of slavery into territory that would eventually become new states. In this agreement slavery was banned in all territories north of latitude 36° 30', except in the state of Missouri.

By 1833 England declared slavery illegal in its West Indies colony, a group of islands between North and South America—not far off the American coast. France was also moving to outlaw slavery.

Many people wondered, would America, the largest slaveholding nation in the world, be the next country to declare slavery illegal?

The North Wasn't Threatened

The North and South, together, created a prosperous America. This prosperity was generated by everyone's hard work, including the work of African slaves.

Many Northerners came to realize slavery was wrong and called for its abolishment. The end of slavery, however, would not hurt the North. When black people needed jobs, they could work in northern factories. If they did, factory owners would have an even larger supply of men, women, and children willing to work for low wages.

In the South, the end of slavery would mean that plantation owners would be setting free the only workers they had. Farmers with thousands of acres and no field-workers would find it extremely difficult to manage their plantations.

LOPSIDED LAWS

In 1840 the total population of the United States was 17,063,357. Of this total, 9,728,920 people lived in northern states, compared to only 7,334,437 people living in the South. Who cares? Well, if you were a Southerner in 1840, you cared a great deal.

In Congress there are two law-making branches, the Senate and the House of Representatives. The number of representatives each state gets to send to Congress depends on how many people live in that state. The larger the state population, the more representatives a state can send to Washington and the more votes that state has to help choose the laws it likes best.

In 1840 the northern states had forty-eight more representatives than the southern states did. Northern representatives could develop laws favoring northern states, and southern representatives could do nothing about it. They were outnumbered—and they didn't like it. Southerners began losing faith in Congress's ability to make laws that served all the people, not just those people living in northern states.

I THOUGHT WE WERE FRIENDS

Southern plantation owners were angry at northern abolitionists for condemning slavery. Since the 1700s, northern and southern colonists worked and fought as patriots and friends against the British to create the United States of America. Northern colonists bought southern crops, timber, and cotton to make their lives more comfortable even though slaves produced these goods. Yet northern abolitionists hated slavery. It was confusing. Perhaps the following story will help simplify the matter:

Johnny and Billy wanted to build a tree house. Johnny, who knew a lot about gardening, began pruning the dead maple tree branches. Billy, who knew a lot about building, gathered up scrap lumber from his garage.

Unfortunately, Billy had only enough wood to build the tree house floor. Billy and Johnny's parents agreed the boys should raise the money they needed to buy the lumber to finish the tree house.

Johnny suggested they harvest apples from the apple tree. Billy thought that was a great idea. Then he looked at the tree. There were apples everywhere, too many apples for two boys to pick. Johnny wasn't worried. He had a plan. He was going to make his younger sister help them. Billy could force his younger brother to help as well.

Billy wasn't so sure about this plan. "If they help us earn the money to build the tree house, don't they have the right to use it?"

"Are you kidding?!" said Johnny. "My sister and your brother are our slaves, not our equals. Besides, think about it, do you really want them in our tree house?"

"No," stated Billy.

"Enough said," said Johnny.

The plan worked. The younger siblings obeyed their older brothers' orders. The apples were harvested. The two boys made enough money to finish constructing their tree house. Everything was perfect. Or was it?

Billy got upset when his younger brother wanted to use the tree house. Billy told Johnny. Johnny revealed that his sister also wanted to use the tree house. "I told her to get lost," said Johnny.

"I think we should let them in," suggested Billy.

"Okay," said Johnny. "I tell you what. We'll buy them a piece of candy instead. That will satisfy them."

"That's still not fair," said Billy, getting annoyed at his friend.

"I thought we were friends," said Johnny.

"We are!" Billy replied.

"We are?" questioned Johnny. "I thought we agreed not to let my sister and your brother use our tree house."

"We should have picked the apples ourselves," sighed Billy.

"That would have taken too long," Johnny reminded him.

"I still say they have the right to use our tree house," insisted Billy.

"Well, not *my* tree house," charged Johnny.

"It's my tree house, too," said Billy.

"Tell you what," said Johnny. "We'll divide the tree house in half. I'll do what I want in my half."

"And I'll do what I want in my half," answered Billy.

"Fine," declared Johnny, "and if that doesn't work, I'll take the tree house for myself."

"Not without a fight," snapped Billy.

Johnny and the southern plantation owners thought the same way. Neither understood what was wrong with forcing people to work for them. Billy and the abolitionists thought that even though they benefited from slavery, it was wrong and should be stopped. Johnny felt Billy had betrayed him. Southerners felt abolitionists had betrayed them.

Almost All Men (and No Women)

The Declaration of Independence, written in 1776, declared that all men were created equal. In 1787 delegates representing twelve of the thirteen states created the United States Constitution. This document determined how our new nation would govern the people.

The Constitution declared that a slave was equal to three fifths of a free man. This allowed southern states to partially count, rather than completely ignore, their slave population when determining the number of representatives a southern state could send to the Congress.

White women were not reduced to a fraction, but they weren't given full rights either. The Constitution gave states the power to deny women the right to vote. The Constitution also allowed southern states to deny slaves the opportunity to own land, to vote, or to receive an education.

Freedom for a Boy of Color

Six-year-old James Thomas and his mother, Sally, were loaded into a wagon. Over bumpy country roads they went, from Nashville, Tennessee, to Charlottesville, Virginia, to a new master. Soon after, he decided to sell them. Back they went to Nashville, the town of James's birth. The year was 1833.

Badly shaken by the experience, Sally feared that she and James would be sold again. She needed help. She could not turn to James's father, John Catron. Everyone knew Catron, a white judge who sat on the Nashville court. He was headed for the U.S. Supreme Court and would not claim his black child. (James carried the last name of Charles Thomas, who had owned Sally when he was born.)

Ephraim Foster, a white farmer, learned that Sally could buy her son's freedom for $400. The price was unusually high. But Sally knew she would pay it. She had bought freedom for her two older sons, and she would do the same for James.

Sally was a laundress. With careful planning, she had saved most of the $400. Farmer Foster loaned her the rest. Then he bought James Thomas and gave Sally her son's freedom papers.

But his freedom ended quickly. A Tennessee law said that freed blacks must leave the state. James was only seven years old, too young to leave his mother. She put him to work in her laundry.

For the next five years, James delivered clean clothes, chopped and hauled firewood, made soap, and ran errands. On winter days when he wasn't needed, he attended school in an integrated, one-room schoolhouse.

James Learns a Trade

In 1842 James was fifteen. He set out for the busy port city of New Orleans. On the public square in the heart of town, he apprenticed to a barber. James possessed a talent for clipping hair, and customers appreciated his intelligence and good manners. Five years later, he returned to Nashville. Tall, slender, and handsome, James was ready to open his own barbershop.

For ten years, James operated a first-class barbershop in Nashville. He trimmed the beards and mustaches of Nashville's important politicians and businessmen. Talk of money and politics filled his shop all day long. Determined to succeed in a white man's world, James said little but heard much. He saw the unequal treatment black people experienced, and he considered himself fortunate.

James charged 15¢ for a haircut and 20¢ for a shave. He was saving money. Andrew Polk, a cousin to President James Polk, asked James to travel with him as his personal servant. James worried about leaving his business. "Don't tell me about your business," Polk said. "I'll buy it and shut it up."

For nearly three years, James traveled with Polk through the North. He attended social events he would never forget. But he was barred from a museum, and once he was ordered out of a theater. White people shouted insults at him. He resented the way he was treated in the North, where people claimed to believe in equality. In the South, blacks might not be treated equally, but they were accepted and they knew what to expect.

Freedom Comes Again

Back in Nashville, James wanted his freedom again, and he believed that he deserved it. He visited Ephraim Foster, the farmer who had helped his mother. Foster went to the county courthouse and requested that James, an adult now, be granted freedom. He declared that his black friend had a good trade and was "industrious, honest, moral, humble, and polite." He said that as a free man, James would "make a valuable, honest, and excellent citizen." In March 1851 the court granted Foster's request.

James could now speak for himself. He asked the court if he, "James Thomas, a free man of Color," could remain in Tennessee, where he was born and where he had a business. The court said yes.

Four years later, in 1855, James moved to St. Louis, Missouri. Like Tennessee, Missouri was a slave state. Land prices were rising quickly, and James bought and sold property, making thousands of dollars. He became a partner in an exclusive St. Louis barbershop. His business skills, money, and manners made him an important black city leader.

In 1868 he married Antoinette Rutgers, a wealthy, young, free black woman. They had a large, lavish wedding. In 1872 their son Arend James was born. They adopted several more children and moved across the Missouri River to raise their children in the Illinois countryside. By 1880 the Thomases had nearly half a million dollars. They were one of the richest black families in America.

Playing on the Plantation

On plantations, most young black children were allowed to play instead of work in the fields. Black and white children swam, fished, had races, learned from each other, and got into mischief stealing from the henhouse and peppering adults' chewing tobacco.

When black children became teenagers, they were forced into a life of slavery. They were not allowed to attend school. Playing between whites and blacks was over. White teenagers were masters, not friends. Whites made the rules blacks had to follow or be punished.

Young slave children played games that many children still play today. Charlie Davenport, a black child on a Mississippi plantation, recalled, "Us played together in de street what run de length o' de quarters. Us th'owed horse shoes, jumped poles, walked on stilts, an' played marbles."

They "played lots of games, like rolly hole. There were two holes and you try to roll a ball in one hole," remembered Tom Johnson, another black child on a plantation in South Carolina. Hanna Davidson, who lived on a Kentucky plantation, recalled a game called Anti-Over. "Six of us would stay on one side of the house and six on the other side. Then we'd throw the ball over the roof. If you'd catch it you'd run around to the other side and hit somebody then start over."

Before and after the Civil War, black and white children played games such as Goosie, Goosie, Gander; I Spy; and Hide-and-Seek. To slave children, these games were also educational. Playing Hide-and-Seek meant the children must know how to count. Because slaves weren't allowed to go to school, white children taught them to count to one hundred. And during ball games, white children added to the fun by reciting lessons they learned in school. Slave children used these opportunities to learn as much as they could.

I SPY

I Spy can be played almost anywhere. To begin, one player picks something everyone can see. The player says, "I spy with my little eyes . . ." The player provides several clues describing the item. Whoever guesses the item becomes the next player. If everyone is stumped, the same player goes again.

In this selection, Charlie Davenport's words have been written down the way the person who interviewed him heard them.

You can play the Ring Dance game, too. Find an outdoor or indoor area of open space large enough for a circle of friends. Before playing Ring Dance, collect various rhythms you can use in your game.

HIDE-AND-SEEK

One player covers his or her eyes and counts out loud to a certain number. Everyone else finds a hiding place. When the player says the last number, he or she begins the search, saying, "One, two, three, I see . . ." When the player has found someone, that person must run to a safe base everyone has agreed upon. If the player tags the person before reaching the base, that person is "it." If no one is tagged, the player must close his or her eyes and start over.

Can you make this game more challenging? Here's a suggestion: the person can ask a player who successfully reaches base to answer a Civil War question. If the player answers the question incorrectly, he or she is "it."

HOW SELLA MARTIN LEARNED TO READ

Sella Martin was a black slave working as a boatman at a hotel in Georgia, Alabama. Sella Martin was poor, but he used his marble-shooting skill to acquire an enormous stockpile of marbles. In the following story, Martin recalls how the game of marbles helped him learn to read.

"There was a white boy who belonged to the hotel, and [because] he was a poor marble player and rather low in stock, he proposed to go in partnership with me. This was just what I had tried to get older white boys to do before, but they were either ashamed of having a slave-boy for a partner, or else they coveted my large stock of marbles. . . . Now I knew that this boy, Eaton Bass, only wished my partnership that he might have a banker upon whom to draw, as he was constantly getting 'broke.' But as I had designs against him quite as selfish, I readily consented to the terms of partnership. He had no stock to begin with, and therefore, I insisted on his putting in an equivalent in the way of service to me, which service was to teach me the alphabet.

"He resisted this enticement for some days, for young as he was, he had been taught by his parents that he was not to teach a slave to read. . . . After three or four days the partnership was solemnly formed by his giving me one of his books as my own, and teaching me my first lesson."

And that is how Sella Martin learned to read.

GOOSIE, GOOSIE, GANDER

The players sit in a circle. One (a goosie) walks around the outside of the circle, tapping each seated person and saying, "Goosie." At any time, however, this person can tap someone and say, "Gander." When this happens, the gander chases the goosie, trying to tag him or her. If the goosie makes it back to where the gander was seated before being tagged, the goosie is safe. The gander now becomes a goosie and must choose a new gander. If the goosie is caught, he or she must play again.

RING DANCES

A very popular game among slave girls, besides playing with dolls and playing house, was Ring Dance. The girls drew a large ring on the dirt. Everyone got into the ring and danced to a variety of assorted rhythmic hand clapping.

It wasn't unusual during this game for black children to criticize whites in songs.

> *"My old mistress promised me,*
> *Before she dies she would set me free.*
> *Now she's dead and gone to hell.*
> *I hope the devil will burn her well."*

Marvelous Marbles

The most popular game on the plantation was marbles—an amusement children have been playing for 2,000 years. Marbles was a game both poor and rich children could play. It was a wonderful opportunity for slave children, especially for slave boys, who played marbles more often than girls. In the game of marbles, any boy, black or white, had the chance to be a champion.

BRING ON YOUR MARBLES

Most American children play a marble game known as Ringer. You can play, too. All you need are thirteen small marbles or other objects; some larger marbles, or shooters, for each player; and a stick or piece of chalk.

The object of the game is to hit the smaller marbles out of the circle, or ring, with your shooter. The first player who hits seven marbles outside the ring is the winner.

The game of Ringer has many rules. Here are the basic instructions:

1. Draw a 10-foot ring on the ground. Draw an *X* in the center, 9 by 9 inches.

2. Place one marble in the center of the *X* and three marbles on each section of the *X*, 3 inches apart.

3. To launch your shooter, make a fist so that at least one knuckle is touching the ground. This is called "knuckling down." Place the shooter on your forefinger and against your thumb. Flicking the thumb forward will propel the shooter toward the object marble.

4. Players may not raise their shooting hand from the ground; this is called "histing." No player can smooth the ground or remove any obstacles. If you break these rules, you lose a turn. If a player slips while shooting, the player can call "slips" and go again. You cannot change your shooter. Any player changing his or her shooter must forfeit the game.

5. A player starts from anywhere outside the ring. When a player hits a small marble outside the ring, that marble is kept by the player. The player goes again. If the shooter has stopped inside the ring, the player shoots again from that spot. If the shooter stops outside the ring, the player can place it anywhere on or beyond the ring. If a player misses, that player removes his or her shooter, and it is the next player's turn. The game ends when one player has seven marbles.

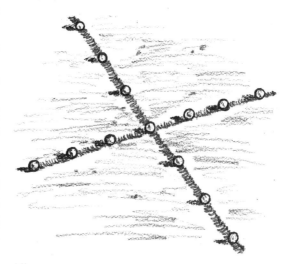

MAKE A SET

With modeling clay that you bake at a very low temperature in your oven at home, you can design and make your own set of marbles. Because modeling clay varies, follow the package directions. By cutting small strips of several colors and kneading them together, you can create unique marble patterns.

Roll the clay in the palms of your hands to shape them as round as you can. Make as many as you like. For a set of marbles that is uniform in size, be sure to use the same amount of clay for each one. And remember that imperfections are part of the charm of handmade marbles.

Ask a grown-up to help you bake your marbles. After they cool, they can be varnished for a clear, high-gloss finish. Check the clay package for advice about safe brands of varnish to use. Be sure to store your marbles in a safe place, where young children can't reach them.

Plantation Life:

AS CHILDREN

Will the slave go free? Or will the slave owner keep the slave? Play this game and find out. For the slave to win, the slave must reach the "Free" section on square 30 and draw the correct "Runaway" card. For the slave owner to win, the slave owner must reach the "Keep Slave" section on square 30. On a plantation, slave owners had the advantage over slaves. In "Plantation Life" this is also true. The rules are designed to give the slave owner a greater opportunity to win.

You Will Need:

A die; two markers (1-inch cardboard circles); three index cards, cut in half. On one marker, write, *SLAVE*. On the other, write, *SLAVE OWNER*. To create the "Runaway" cards, take five of the half-cards and write one of the following statements on the lined side of each. Shuffle them and spread them out, written-side down.

You make your way to Canada without your family.

You're captured and whipped. *Go back to square 12.*

You're captured and whipped. *Go back to square 15.*

You're captured and whipped. *Go back to square 19.*

The slave owner grants your freedom.

1 Hot day. You go swimming in the creek. *Move ahead three spaces.*

2 You win all the marbles. *Move ahead five spaces.*

3 You're easily found during a game of Hide-and-Seek. Someone had to be peeking.

4 You catch a fish and barbecue it for lunch!

5 You're caught stealing chickens. *Move back one space.*

6 You win a wrestling match. *Move ahead one space.*

7 Boating race ends in a tie. *Roll again.*

8 You set the pigs free. *Move back four spaces.*

9 You spend the morning picking berries. Yum!

10 You lose seven marbles during a game. *Move back one space.*

11 You spend the afternoon playing Fox and Hounds.

12 You play with a slave's ball made of yarn and covered in a sock. The white children laugh.

13 You have a great time walking on stilts!

AS SLAVE OWNER/ SLAVE

You feel sick and sit in the shade. You're whipped. *Move back one space and lose a turn.*

14 You find a slave, who should be working, sitting in the shade. *Move ahead two spaces.*

You're moved into one of the remaining overcrowded huts. No apology is given.

15 Careless! You start a fire. Half of the slave huts are burned. *Move back four spaces and lose a turn.*

Your sister is working at the master's house. She feels like part of their family.

16 You complain to your mother about the house servants chatting too much.

17 Your tutor teaches you French.

You are caught looking at a newspaper in the barn. *Move back two spaces.*

A Board Game

18 You act impolitely at a party. Your parents are embarrassed. *Move back one space.*

You catch a huge catfish with your father. Move ahead two spaces.

19 You have a great time at church.

You sing hymns beneath the magnolia trees with other slave families.

20 You give away your new clothes, which you hate, to a slave. Parents find out! *Lose a turn.*

You win a gambling game. Move ahead three spaces.

21 You whip a slave for disobeying you. *Move ahead two spaces.*

Your aunt faints in the field. You refuse to leave her. You're whipped. Lose a turn.

24 Your parents give you greater responsibilities. *Move ahead three spaces.*

The overseer praises your hard work. Move ahead two spaces.

23 You celebrate your twentieth birthday.

Your brother dies at age seven.

22 Record cotton harvest. Family profits soar.

Record harvest. The master offers his thanks and gives you extra food.

25 A horse kicks you. You break several ribs. Your mother nurses you.

Your arm is damaged in a cotton gin. You can't work. The master is angry. Move back three spaces.

26 You're getting married. Your parents are pleased that the family is wealthy. *Move ahead one space.*

Your father is sold to another plantation.

29 Sunday: A day of rest.

Sunday: A day of rest.

28 Your father celebrates his forty-fifth birthday.

Your mother celebrates her twenty-ninth birthday. She misses her husband.

27 You dream of being a master/mistress of the plantation, and oversleep. *Lose a turn.*

You dream of escape. Move ahead three spaces.

30 Keep Slave

Free

How You Play:

1. Place the markers in a bag. Each player chooses one. The slave owner rolls the die first. On the first roll only, the slave owner moves both the slave owner and the slave marker. If the square says to move ahead or roll again, he or she should do so, moving both markers until the turn is over. Now it is the slave's turn. For the rest of the game, the slave owner and the slave alternate turns, unless a player loses a turn.

2. From square 14 on, the slave owner reads the top portion of each square. The slave reads the bottom half.

3. The slave owner doesn't need to roll an exact number to land on the "Keep Slave" section. The slave MUST roll the exact number to land on the "Free" section. If the slave lands on the "Free" section, he or she chooses one card from the "Runaway" cards and follows the directions. The slave owner reshuffles the cards for the next drawing.

4. If both players are asked to lose a turn, the slave owner takes the next turn.

Cornered in the Canebrake

Taking careful aim at the puma, Jacob fired.

Jacob and Perry had hunted all day on the east Texas prairie. Their ponies were tired, and night was falling. But neither boy wanted to return home to Ma and Polly without even an old jackrabbit for the soup kettle.

"Jacob," Perry said, "let's ride round that cane thicket. Maybe we'll scare up a turkey."

Jacob, two years younger than Perry, hesitated. "That's the wrong way," he argued. "Ma'll be worried if we aren't back soon. Besides, our ammunition is running low."

"Oh, phooey," Perry teased. "If we don't see anything right away, we'll head straight home. You're just afraid to go near the canebrake."

"You don't know anything," Jacob muttered. Perry touched his spur to Fleetwind's sweaty side. Pony and rider raced ahead in the dusk. Reluctantly, Jacob spurred his horse, Goldenbell, and caught up to his brother.

At the edge of the dense canebrake, the boys stopped. A narrow trail led into the cane. The reeds stood twelve feet tall. At their full height of twenty-five feet, their tops would bend, forming a dense cover that would block out the daylight. Pa had often warned them about getting lost in the canebrake.

"Perry," Jacob said again, "I'm going home." As he spoke, they heard reeds snap inside the thicket. Without a word, Perry and his pony started down the trail. Annoyed, Jacob watched his brother disappear into the dense brush. He would have to wait. He wouldn't go home alone.

Jacob was caught in the middle again. Perry always wanted to ride farther than they should or cross a river at its rapids. Since Pa had died last winter, Ma depended on her sons to run the farm and hunt. The Texas colonists helped each other, but Jacob knew his family had to take care of itself. Suddenly his brother's voice called out.

"Jacob!" Perry shouted from the canebrake. "Help me!"

"I'm coming!" Jacob yelled back. He snapped his pony's reins and started into the thicket. But he couldn't see down the dark trail. It was only a narrow path of short, hard stubble. Broken cane stalks rubbed against his legs. Goldenbell struggled forward. Perry couldn't have gone very far at this speed, Jacob thought with relief. He caught sight of his brother's pony, Fleetwind, when Perry screamed.

"Jacob!" Perry's wail was followed by the deep, angry cry of a cat. Fleetwind snorted. The cane cracked and snapped, as a small deer bolted, brushing against Fleetwind as it tried to escape. A second vicious snarl rang out. Jacob watched Fleetwind rise up in fear, throwing Perry backward from the saddle.

Perry hit the canes and slid to the ground as Fleetwind tried to back into the thicket. With a tight grip on Goldenbell's reins, Jacob yelled to Perry to roll out of the pony's way. Whimpering with pain, Perry dragged himself to safety. Then Jacob spotted the majestic brown puma, crouching over a fallen deer.

The huge cat rose, its eyes on Jacob. Jacob's frightened pony tried to back away as Fleetwind had. He squeezed his legs tightly around the pony. He raised his rifle, trying to calm his trembling hands. The rifle held one lead ball. Taking careful aim at the puma, Jacob fired.

The huge cat yelped, jerked, and dropped. Jacob watched the bleeding animal slump over the deer. The boy paused an instant before reloading. He waited, watching for signs of life from the puma. He fired a second shot into the neck of the huge cat, then slid off his pony. His legs were weak as he approached the animal.

Jacob stood for a moment, staring at the puma. Now he would go home with meat for his family and the beautiful skin of the puma for himself. It would make a fine blanket for his bed.

Jacob turned to help his brother. Somehow he must load Perry onto the saddle behind him, track down Fleetwind, and hoist the deer and the puma onto the pony's back. Ma and Polly would wait several more hours for their boys. But in a way, he thought, he was glad he had entered the canebrake.

The Land Called Them

In 1820 a large group of Missourians and their slaves loaded their furniture and belongings into wagons and followed Stephen F. Austin into Texas. When these first families arrived, they settled in an area approved for them by the Mexican government, in a region between the Colorado and Neches Rivers. Families clustered in small settlements, building their sturdy log cabins or sod homes, planting cotton in the rich soil, and living uneasily among the native Karankawas. Many of the earliest settlements failed, but the small Austin colony San Felipe, founded on a prairie near the banks of the Brazos River, survived.

A few years later, nearly 8,000 Americans who had heard about the vast lands and good soil had moved into Texas. Refusing to limit slavery or follow other laws of Mexico, they formed their own government, the Republic of Texas.

Letters on a Wire

Before 1837 Americans communicated by writing letters to each other. These letters took weeks to arrive at their destinations. In 1837 that all changed.

Samuel Morse invented the telegraph. The telegraph allowed people to send and receive messages in a few hours rather than waiting weeks.

Morse's invention took a message, translated it into a series of dots and dashes known as the Morse code, and sent this coded message over a wire charged with electricity. The received message was translated back into words. By 1860 people were getting their news the same day events happened.

SLAVES IN TEXAS

In 1803 President Thomas Jefferson bought a huge piece of land—the Louisiana Territory—from France. This territory stretched from the west bank of the Mississippi River to the Gulf of Mexico and to the Rocky Mountains. The land beyond the Louisiana Territory, from the Rockies to the Pacific Ocean, was claimed by Spain.

American trappers, hunters, explorers, and settlers spread into the Louisiana Territory and beyond. Some of them formed friendships with Spanish and Mexican leaders in the Far West. One of these "diplomats" was Moses Austin, a lead miner from Missouri. Spanish authorities gave him a land grant and allowed him to bring a colony of Americans to settle in the Providence of Texas. But before his colony arrived, Mexico became independent from Spain, and Moses Austin died. His son, however, carried out his dream. In 1820 Stephen Austin led 300 American settlers and their slaves into Texas.

The Mexicans welcomed the settlers but disapproved of owning slaves. In 1829 the Mexican Congress abolished slavery as most other countries in the world had done. The Congress told the American settlers they could keep the slaves they had, but no more could be brought in. The unhappy settlers protested. Calling themselves Texans, they began talking about forming their own republic and making their own laws.

The Texans' talk of independence grew into an armed rebellion against Mexico. In 1836 all 187 Texan soldiers were killed in San Antonio, at the Battle of the Alamo. A few weeks later, led by Sam Houston, the Texans struck back at the Mexican army and captured General Santa Anna. Mexico surrendered, and Texans declared their freedom. They formed the Republic of Texas and made Houston their first president.

MORE TROUBLE WITH MEXICO

On December 29, 1845, Texas became the twenty-eighth state in the Union. The citizens voted to allow slavery. Mexico and the United States did not agree about the location of the border that marked their countries. President James Polk sent soldiers to the Rio Grande to build a fort on the Texas side. Across the river, Mexican soldiers watched angrily as the building went up. In May 1846 the soldiers began arguing. Shouts turned into gunfire, and President Polk declared war against Mexico. The Mexican War is sometimes called the "Forgotten War." It was fought on lands most Americans knew very little about and lasted a year and a half, until Mexico surrendered.

The war ended with the signing of the Treaty of Guadalupe Hidalgo in 1848. The United States paid Mexico $15 million and received 523,000 square miles of land, stretching from the Texas border to the Pacific Ocean. This territory would later become several new states. During this period, President Polk added other land to the United States, too. In 1845 he received a part of the Oregon Country, from the Columbia River stretching north to 49 degrees latitude, from Great Britain. With these new western territories, a vast stretch of land extending from the Atlantic to the Pacific Ocean now belonged to the United States.

H IS FOR HENRY BIBB

Henry Bibb, a slave, ran away from his master to live as a free man with his family in Canada. In 1844 he wrote to his former slave owner, William Gatewood. In his letter he recalled painful moments. Bibb wrote, "To be compelled to stand by and see you whip and slash my wife without mercy, when I could afford her no protection, not even by offering myself to suffer the lash in her place, was more than I felt it to be the duty of a slave husband to endure.... My infant child was also frequently flogged by Mrs. Gatewood, for crying, until its skin was bruised literally purple. This kind of treatment was what drove me from home and family, to a seek a better home for them. But I am willing to forget the past. I should be pleased to hear from you again . . . if it should be agreeable to yourself. I subscribe myself a friend to the oppressed, and Liberty forever."

Harriet the Runaway

By moonlight, Harriet drove for three nights.

Harriet Tubman was easy to recognize, and a lot of people wanted her captured. The small black woman—an escaped slave—had an ugly scar on her forehead and most of her teeth were missing. She carried a small bottle of paregoric, medicine that would quiet crying babies. She also carried a loaded pistol. Harriet believed she had a right to be free, and she had decided that she would prefer death to life as a slave. The reward for the capture of this small runaway woman was $12,000!

As a slave child born in Maryland, Harriet was cruelly treated. When her master died, she and her brothers were sold to a slave trader in Georgia. On the morning in 1849 when the new master came to the plantation to get her, Harriet was missing. She had sneaked away, alone in the night. She slept in the woods; rode in a wagon; walked beside a river; hid in a barn, a haystack, and a potato hole; and finally reached Philadelphia. She got a job as a cook and made friends with other black people who told her about the Underground Railroad.

Two years after her escape, she sneaked back to Maryland and rescued her sister and brother-in-law. She found them huddled inside an auction pen at a courthouse, waiting to be sold.

Later she returned to Maryland and brought her brothers to freedom. This time she took a large group of slaves all the way to Canada, where they could not be captured. Then she returned to the South. Soon people were calling her "Moses," a reminder of the biblical prophet who led the Israelites out of Egypt.

Harriet put her life at risk, time and again. Her faith in God gave her courage; her sharp sense of danger alerted her to traps. The reward for her capture went higher.

Somebody's Stealing the Bread

Matthew McKeever knew how to keep a secret. So when he agreed to hide eight slaves on his farm, he kept it to himself. For four weeks, the runaway blacks hid in his barn, up in the sheep loft. His neighbor, John Jordan, came over to feed the slaves extra food cooked right in Mrs. McKeever's kitchen. Meals and beverages were stored in the spring house, a small building that sat over a natural spring, where milk and foods were stored at cool temperatures.

McKeever had a big family and lots of workers on his farm. But no one detected the hidden slaves. The hired girl, however, knew something peculiar was going on. "Somebody's stealing the bread," she reported to Mrs. McKeever.

But Harriet wasn't finished. There were two important people she thought about night and day. Her mother and father, both slaves, were very old. They could not wade through swamps or sleep in forests at night. To rescue them, Harriet needed a different plan.

In June of 1857, she rode a train back to Maryland. Wearing a big sunbonnet and carrying live chickens from the market, she returned to the plantation of her childhood, as though she had been shopping that day. Her parents were overjoyed when she sneaked into their cabin that night and said she had returned to rescue them. They agreed to go north with her. Harriet disappeared. Within two hours she was back, with a stolen horse and wagon.

Daring to travel the public roads by moonlight, Harriet drove for three nights. Once they reached Philadelphia, they could travel freely the rest of the way. It was Harriet's most risky—yet her easiest—rescue ever. With some of her money, Harriet bought her parents a house in Auburn, New York. They lived there for the rest of their lives.

For two more years she traveled back and forth, helping others escape. In 1858 she began speaking in public. People were amazed by her stories of danger and dedication. The money she made from speaking bought supplies to help more blacks reach safety.

Harriet Tubman became the most famous conductor on the Underground Railroad. The reward for her capture rose to $40,000. Yet no one would turn her in. She helped nearly 400 slaves reach freedom. But in 1860, war was in the air. It was time to stop. Soon Harriet would be needed as a nurse.

SECRET WALLS AND HIDDEN HALLS

In the 1830s, railroads and trains were the marvel of America. As tracks spread across the land, people could travel more cheaply, faster, and farther. Hundreds of daring slaves traveled, too, but not in comfort or style. Desperate and proud, they stole away in the night, risking their lives to reach one of the "free" states. These were in the North, where slavery was against the law.

The escape routes taken by runaway slaves became known as the Underground Railroad. This name may have been used for the first time in 1831, with the disappearance of a slave named Tice Davids.

As more slaves made the run toward freedom, they were secretly aided by free blacks and by whites who hated slavery. There were never any real trains or tracks, but helpers were called conductors, and hideouts were called stations.

The helpers offered food, money, and supplies, or their barns or houses for shelter. They built secret walls, hidden hallways, and revolving bookcases that led to backyard escape routes. They planned ways to signal—such as lantern lights in windows—if it was safe to approach the house, or when to hide from slave-hunting men who combed the countryside.

For slaves to escape, they depended on each

Harriet Tubman

other. They traded information about hiding in the woods by day and traveling north by following certain stars at night. Slaves walked hundreds of miles to gain their freedom, and even left the United States to live in Canada or Mexico. Running away to freedom was scary and dangerous. Those who risked it knew they might never see their families or friends again.

Dreaming of a Train

The *L. L. Robinson* was the locomotive of the Sacramento Valley Line Railroad. The *Robinson* ran twenty-two miles from Sacramento to Folsom. To create California's first railroad, iron rails and other material were transported by ship around the horn of South America. It took seven months to complete the railroad at a cost of $1,380,000.

To most Americans it was a crazy idea—building a transcontinental railroad linking America's Pacific and Atlantic Coasts. If it wasn't crazy, then it was impossible. There was no way a railroad could be built through the snow-capped, mighty mountains of the West.

Besides, what was the point? Most Americans thought the land west of the Rocky Mountains was a desert fit only for savages and prairie dogs.

But Californians longed for a faster way to travel east to the Atlantic states. They imagined getting on a train in Sacramento and getting off in Philadelphia only days later. That was much better than taking a steamship from San Francisco to Central America, transferring to another ship at the Isthmus of Panama, and then on to a destination on the Atlantic Coast. This route took six weeks!

Theodore Judah, a railroad engineer, was driven by this dream of a transcontinental railroad. It was a dream so big, so alive, it followed him all day and slept with him all night. "It will be built, and I'm going to have something to do with it," he vowed. How often Anna Judah heard her husband make this claim.

In 1854 Judah moved closer to his dream. "Anna, I'm going to California to be the pioneer railroad engineer of the Pacific Coast!" said the twenty-seven-year-old Judah. Anna Judah wasn't smiling. In six years her husband's engineering jobs had forced them to move twenty times. And now to California!

In 1855 the Sacramento Valley Railroad was born. Judah had done it! He had engineered California's first railroad. Californians welcomed the sight of a train shooting smoke plumes into the blue sky and the feel of the ground trembling beneath them as the locomotive *L. L. Robinson* and its cars passed by.

But Judah was hardly satisfied with this achievement. It was just the start. To him, a transcontinental railroad would be the finish line.

First he needed to find a route that would allow a train to travel east from Sacramento up through the Sierra Nevada mountains and down to the Great Basin of Nevada. There, Californians would connect with the Union Pacific Railroad and continue eastward, eventually reaching the Atlantic states.

Now, this route couldn't be just any old trail. It had to be on solid ground and rise gradually over the mountains. Judah wouldn't be able to design the bridges and other structures needed if the route had too many twists and turns or changed elevation too quickly.

For the next six years Judah surveyed the Sierra. He gathered information, wrote articles for the *Sacramento Union* about his dream and his findings, and tirelessly went before Congress asking for money to fund his railroad project.

In 1860 Judah received a letter from Dr. Daniel Strong. Dr. Strong said he had found a route for Judah's railroad. He had located an abandoned

Theodore Judah, a railroad engineer, was driven by the dream of a transcontinental railroad.

Riding a Nightmare

It may have been a dream to build a transcontinental railroad, but it was a nightmare to ride one of its trains. Passengers traveling from Omaha, Nebraska, to San Francisco, California, had to endure a hard four-and-a-half-day journey, traveling at twenty miles an hour.

The ride was bumpy. The train windows constantly rattled. If you opened the windows, dust poured in. If you kept the windows closed, the air was impossibly stuffy. Temperatures drastically shifted as the train went from hot flatlands to cold mountains back to hot valleys.

The scenery was often barren and boring, unless it happened to be on fire, as drifting sparks from the passing locomotive ignited dry prairie grass. For entertainment, gun-carrying passengers shot at deer or buffalo during the day.

wagon road in the canyons of the Donner Lake area near Dutch Flat. Judah went to see this amateur surveyor.

The two men made their way on horseback into the mountains north of Lake Tahoe through forests of Jeffrey pines, red fir, white pines, and wildflowers. Blue jays swooped and bald eagles floated on the cool wind currents above them.

Dr. Strong suddenly pulled on the reins of his horse and directed Judah to follow him on foot.

Ahead, they stared at a mountain ridge lined with trees. The long ridge steadily rose to the mountain's peak at Donner Summit, 7,042 feet above sea level. At the end of the ridge the old wagon trail angled southeast to the Truckee River valley and onto the flats of the Great Basin. Could this be Judah's route? He wouldn't know for sure until he studied his maps of the area.

That night, the two men were surprised by a snowstorm. Judah and Strong had spent so much time exploring they had forgotten about the change of season. They had to leave, or risk being buried in the falling snow. In the darkness, they hurriedly broke camp and desperately searched until they found the trail.

Cold, wet, and exhausted, they followed the trail to the foothill town of Dutch Flat, where Dr. Strong owned a drugstore. Judah didn't rest. He went into the store, stretched his maps and profiles on the counter, and verified his observations. He said, "This route is more favorable for a railroad over the Sierra Nevada than any other one which has been examined by engineers. . . . No serious engineering difficulties present themselves."

Judah had found his route. He and Dr. Strong formed a new partnership called the Central Pacific Railroad Company.

Judah had located the railroad route. Now he

Through Indian Lands

In order to create the transcontinental railroad, tracks had to be built on land sacred to Indian people.

The Sioux and Cheyenne fought the railroad. They attacked railroad workers who slaughtered buffalo for food. To the Indian people, the buffalo offered more than food to eat or skins to turn into clothing and housing. The buffalo was part of Indian life. Children imitated the buffalo. Elders honored the buffalo. It wasn't just an animal. The buffalo was a member of their family. The Indians fought because they feared the railroad would destroy the buffalo and change the land and their way of life forever.

A Never-Ending Job

For five years, the Central Pacific Railroad and the Union Pacific Railroad raced to connect their lines from opposite directions. Finally, in 1869, the tracks met in the West. On May 10, 1869, railroad executives, dignitaries, workers, and reporters gathered to celebrate the completed railway. The lines joined at Promontory Point, Utah, where Leland Stanford drove a golden spike into the last rail. Soon travelers could ride the train from one end of America to the other.

But work on the railways continued. Tracks had to be kept clear of obstacles that could block the train, causing disaster. Fallen trees or boulders, rock slides, and even stray animals could pose danger to a train. Bridges and trestles needed careful inspection to make sure the supports remained strong. In the upper photo, Chinese workers haul earth to fill in a long trestle.

The Dreamer Dies

Theodore Judah was excited about the creation of a transcontinental railroad. The Big Four were excited about making money. They formed their own construction company and paid themselves to construct the railroad. Their construction plan was simple: build quickly and cheaply—and make as large a profit as possible.

Theodore Judah thought their plan shameful. He searched for new investors to buy the railroad company from the Big Four. Eventually he found the necessary investors. Filled with confidence, Judah traveled to New York to meet with them.

Unfortunately, he contracted yellow fever during the journey and died a week after arriving in New York, in 1863. Because of his death, the Big Four remained in control of the Central Pacific Railroad.

needed the money to begin building tracks through the Sierra. A meeting was set up with four wealthy Sacramento men: Leland Stanford, Charles Crocker, Mark Hopkins, and Collis P. Huntington.

Judah didn't talk of his dream. He spoke of profit. Mine owners, farmers, everyone would gladly pay for the right to use the fastest transportation system linking the east and west coasts.

The four men agreed to buy shares in Judah and Dr. Strong's Central Pacific Railroad Company of California. Later they became known as the "Big Four."

One last obstacle remained: the U.S. government. For several years Theodore Judah went before Congress trying to convince the politicians to support a transcontinental railroad. Each time Judah was rejected.

In 1860 Judah went before the Congress again, a congress burdened by the approach of a civil war. It was a terrible time for the nation, but a golden opportunity for Judah and the Big Four.

The impending war changed the transcontinental railroad from a crazy idea to a sensible notion. Building such a railroad would make it easier for the North to protect California and the Nevada Territory, as well as to transport gold and silver from the mines to help finance the war.

Judah's project now appeared vital to the northern states' prosperity and security. Finally, in 1862, the first Pacific Railroad bill was signed, followed by the second bill in 1864.

These two bills authorized the government to give the railroads 130 million acres of land. State governments gave the railroads 49 million acres. This enormous gift of land was larger than the state of Texas. With this gift, the costs of building the railroad could be paid.

African Americans preparing cotton for the gin on a plantation. Port Royal Island, South Carolina.

FOUR RUNAWAY SLAVES

"The boys are gone!" said George to his father.

Four slaves had run away in the night from Edward Gorsuch's Maryland plantation. He felt betrayed. He considered himself a fair slave owner. He made sure his slaves learned the Lord's Prayer and the Commandments. He even set some slaves free on their twenty-eighth birthdays. Gorsuch had planned on setting these four men free. Instead, they had run away. He was determined to get them back. But the year was 1849. The tough Fugitive Slave Act had yet to become law. Gorsuch couldn't expect the government to help capture his slaves.

Gorsuch did what he could. He hired a messenger to find the four men. The messenger carried a letter stating that if the four slaves returned, no harm would come to them. After two years of searching, in August 1851, Gorsuch received word that the runaway slaves were living in Lancaster County, Pennsylvania, somewhere near the town of Christiana.

Gorsuch headed for Pennsylvania with a small band of friends and family, to demand that the fugitive slave commissioner of Philadelphia, Edward Ingraham, seize his slaves. Gorsuch now had the Fugitive Slave Law of 1850 on his side.

Two weary young runaways sat for their portrait in Baton Rouge. During the war that city was federally occupied and became a haven for thousands of runaway slaves.

Many newspapers ran ads offering rewards for the capture of runaway slaves.

THE COMPROMISE OF 1850

American settlers moved to California, Nevada, Utah, the Southwest, and Texas. These territories belonged to Mexico, along with land that today is Arizona, New Mexico, parts of Colorado, and Wyoming. By 1848 America won the war with Mexico and acquired these lands.

To keep a balance between the slave and free states, the Compromise of 1850 determined that Texas would be a slave state and California would be a free state. The fate of the other territories would be decided by the people who settled in each.

The compromise also established a Fugitive Slave Law. Now slave catchers and slave owners could ask a government commissioner to help them capture runaway slaves. Once they were captured, these slaves couldn't defend themselves in a court of law. Anyone hiding or preventing the arrest of a slave would be jailed for up to six months and fined $1,000.

African Americans in the North lived under constant threat of being kidnapped and returned to slavery.

$200 REWARD

Ranaway from the subscriber, on Sunday night, the 16th of December, negro boy Gusty, who calls himself GustavusSimms, he is about twenty years of age, five feet six inches high, dark ginger-bread color, large flat nose, which he almost hides with upper lip when he laughs. He carried away with him one black and one grey coat and a brown over-coat and a pair of drab fulled cloth pants and blue comfort, he also had an oil-cloth clothes bag.

I will pay $50 for his apprehension in the state of Maryland or in the District of Columbia, and $200 if taken in a free State.

ANN P. EVERSFIELD.

Bladensburg Po., Prince George's Co., Md.

The Battle at Christiana

Parker walked right up to Gorsuch.

The following story is based on the documentary account Resistance at Christiana *by Jonathan Katz.*

It was night when William Parker returned home from work. He opened the door. There sat two frightened fugitives, Joshua Kite and Samuel Thompson. They told Parker the news. Edward Gorsuch, their slave owner, was coming with a posse to arrest them. Parker just laughed. "It is all talk," he said.

Parker did not scare easily. As a slave boy in Maryland, he had refused to work in the field one day. The master threatened to beat him. Parker overpowered him and ran away to Pennsylvania to work as a free man.

Parker told Kite and Thompson to relax. It made no difference if a posse was coming or not. No one would take them away.

The next morning there was no sign of a posse. Joshua Kite went to work. He walked down a dirt path and met Edward Gorsuch and the posse, headed by Marshal Kline! Kite ran back to the house and through the open door, yelling, "William! Kidnappers! Kidnappers!"

The posse chased Kite. When they reached Parker's house, Marshal Kline and Gorsuch entered the two-story house. They looked up the staircase leading to the second floor. "Come down," called Gorsuch. "If you come down and go home with me without any trouble, I will overlook the past."

"If you take one of us, you must take us over our dead bodies," called out one of the fugitives.

William Parker looked down at Gorsuch and Kline from the stair landing. Behind him were seven armed black men and women, including Gorsuch's slaves. Parker defiantly asked, "Who are you?"

Kline cautiously leaned against the stairs and answered, "I am the United States marshal."

"I do not care for you or the United States," declared Parker.

Hearing the brazen tone in Parker's voice, Kline stepped back from the stairs. "Yes, I have heard many a Negro talk as big as you," said Kline, trying to sound fearless, "and then have taken him; and I'll take you."

"You have not taken me yet," said Parker.

Marshal Kline decided to read the warrant authorizing him to arrest the runaway slaves. He hoped hearing this legal document would scare Parker.

Parker wasn't frightened. "Go up, Mr. Kline," commanded Gorsuch.

"I am coming," said Kline.

"Well, come on," dared Parker. Kline didn't move.

"You have my property," said Gorsuch to Parker.

The word "property" angered Parker. "Men cannot be property," he declared.

As the standoff continued, Eliza, Parker's wife, blew a horn out the upstairs window to signal friends they were in trouble and needed help. The posse, waiting outside, fired a hail of bullets at the window.

Soon, black reinforcements appeared, armed with rifles, pitchforks, stones, and corn cutters. Those with guns loaded their weapons.

Emboldened by the sight of their friends, Parker and the others came downstairs. Parker stood in the doorway.

"You can't come out here," said Gorsuch.

When news of the battle at Christiana reached Maryland and Gorsuch's neighbors, various reports stated that "the feelings of some have led to a deep-seated and burning desire for revenge."

An anti-slavery newspaper in Lancaster, Pennsylvania, reported, "Gangs of armed ruffians from Maryland, assisted by the lowest ruffians this region can furnish, are prowling around the country . . . arresting indiscriminately [randomly] all colored persons whom they meet."

Southern states throughout the nation demanded that Northerners obey the Fugitive Slave Law or "we will leave you."

"Why?" said Parker. "This is my place."

"If you come out, I will give you the contents of these." Gorsuch waved a pistol in each hand to show he, too, was a bold man.

"Old man, if you don't go away, I will break your neck." Parker stepped out of the doorway and walked right up to Gorsuch.

Marshal Kline feared a fight. He pleaded with Gorsuch to leave. Gorsuch had no intention of retreating. Kline offered a truce to Parker. "If you withdraw your men, I will withdraw mine."

"It is too late," said Parker. Gorsuch had already signaled his men to line up, ready to fight. Parker signaled his fifteen or so comrades to do the same.

"Father, will you take this from a n-gger?" demanded Gorsuch's son, Dickerson.

Parker threatened to knock Dickerson's teeth down his throat. Dickerson fired at Parker, putting a hole in his hat. Parker slapped Dickerson's pistol to the ground. Dickerson ran. Pinckney, Parker's brother-in-law, fired his gun twice, wounding Dickerson.

Samuel Thompson boldly walked up to Gorsuch, his former slave owner. They argued. Thompson snatched Pinckney's gun and swung it against his slave owner. Gorsuch got up and called to his men to fire. Thompson hit Gorsuch again. Gorsuch ignored his pain and stood up. The white men fired their guns. The black men and women charged them. The white men ran away.

Gorsuch was left to defend himself against his black attackers. Parker watched Gorsuch struggle then fall down dead in his yard. Even though William Parker despised slave owners, he admired Gorsuch's bravery. "Old Mr. Gorsuch was the bravest of his party," he said.

"Old Mr. Gorsuch was the bravest of his party."

TAKE YOUR PROPERTY WITH YOU

Dred Scott was a black slave living in the slave state of Missouri. His master was an army doctor named Emerson. Before the Civil War, Dr. Emerson was stationed in both the free state of Illinois and the free territory of Wisconsin. When he was stationed away from home, Dr. Emerson took Dred Scott with him.

After Dr. Emerson died, Dred Scott's white friends in Missouri recommended that he sue to be set free from Mrs. Emerson, who had inherited Scott along with his wife and daughter. Scott's friends believed that since Scott had lived on free soil with Dr. Emerson for long periods of time, the slave should be considered a free man.

For the next eleven years, Scott and his lawyers fought for his freedom right up to the highest court in the nation, the Supreme Court. The court ruled against Dred Scott. They believed that no law could stop Americans from taking their property anywhere they wanted to. Since slaves were property, they could be taken anywhere in the territories.

This decision to deny one man's freedom caused Northerners to feel helpless in stopping slavery. If a slave owner could take his slaves into the territories, these territories could never be free. How could a free territory allow slavery? Northerners felt the decision was "the greatest crime in the [records] of the Republic."

Southerners were pleased by the court's deci-

sion. They believed the right to own slaves was now an indisputable privilege. The court's decision did nothing to calm the tensions between the North and the South.

SLAVERY IS SPREADING!

Imagine that you're holding up a steak in front of two very hungry dogs. You look at the dogs and say, "Be nice to each other and share." Then you drop the steak between them and step back. Now imagine how the two dogs are behaving. Can you see them fighting to determine who gets to eat that steak?

The passing of the Kansas-Nebraska Act, in 1854, pitted pro-slavery and anti-slavery settlers against each other like two dogs—and Kansas was the steak. It was a provocative law. The Kansas-Nebraska Act repealed the Missouri Compromise of 1820, which prohibited slavery in northern territories. Now settlers could decide whether to allow or prohibit slavery in the two new Kansas and Nebraska territories.

Anti-slavery and pro-slavery settlers rushed to Kansas. They tormented and killed each other for the right to determine whether Kansas would be a free or slave state.

Northerners everywhere were outraged by the Kansas-Nebraska Act. They were deeply afraid Congress would repeal other laws prohibiting slavery in the North. Northerners wondered if slavery would be allowed in the free state of Ohio or Michigan. What about New York? Slavery was spreading. Where would it end?

A NEW PARTY

The Kansas-Nebraska Act not only caused settlers to fight each other; it caused politicians to do the same. The Whig party split into the southern and northern Whigs. The southern Whigs, who agreed with the Kansas-Nebraska Act, joined the Democratic party, which also supported slavery in the western territories.

Northern Whigs, abolitionists, Democrats who disagreed with the Kansas-Nebraska Act, and other citizens joined to form the new Republican party. The original Republican party was headed by Thomas Jefferson. The members of this new Republican party believed slavery "was a great, moral, social, and political evil."

The Whig party, split over slavery, was gone forever.

OLD MR. LINCOLN

The August afternoon was a scorcher. In the public square, a brass band played merrily. Red-white-and-blue bunting fluttered from the speakers' platform.

"There goes old Mr. Lincoln," a boy called out as Abraham Lincoln headed for the square. The lawyer from Springfield was forty-seven, but people had been calling him old since he was thirty. They made fun of his sharp features, too. His wife, Mary, answered them this way: "He may not be the most handsome of men, but his heart is big and warm."

Lincoln had come to Ottawa, Illinois, because he had decided to run for the United States Senate. His opponent was the incumbent, Stephen A. Douglas. Lincoln had challenged Douglas to debate him, and this was their first public meeting. By October, they would debate six more times and make dozens of separate speeches.

Stephen Douglas was wealthy, stylish, handsome, and well known—the opposite of Lincoln in many ways. But Lincoln was a lawyer and a confident speaker. His moral character made him argue for what was right over what was popular. People respected both "Long Abe" and the "Little Giant." And the two men spoke highly of each other. But when they debated the issue of slavery, Lincoln won. Lincoln said it was wrong and should be gradually eliminated everywhere. Douglas said the people should decide.

On Election Day, after a close vote, Stephen Douglas was reelected to the Senate. Lincoln was disappointed, but he was glad he had run for office. "I now sink out of view and shall be forgotten," he said. But he believed his ideas would be remembered.

Some weeks after the election, as Lincoln was leaving the courthouse in Bloomington, Illinois, a popular Republican leader named Jess Fell stopped him. Jess Fell told Lincoln, "Now we need you to run for president of the United States. I want you to write your history for me."

Lincoln hesitated. "I admit that I am ambitious, and I would like to be the president. But," he continued, "there is nothing in my early history that would interest you or anybody else." He thanked Fell for the compliment and started down the stairs. As he left, Fell called out, "You must listen, and you must do as I ask."

You have probably read stories about Abraham Lincoln since you began school. Because he changed America from a nation that tolerated slavery into one where the fight for equality for *all* people continues, every American should think about, and celebrate, his life. He was a man of great wisdom and patience, qualities America needed badly in 1861. In his lifetime, many Americans—Northerners and Southerners alike—knew they had found a remarkable leader.

Imagine the United States divided into two countries. Without Lincoln's vision of "one nation," today we might need a passport to visit our friends in neighboring states.

A Few Votes for Whiskers

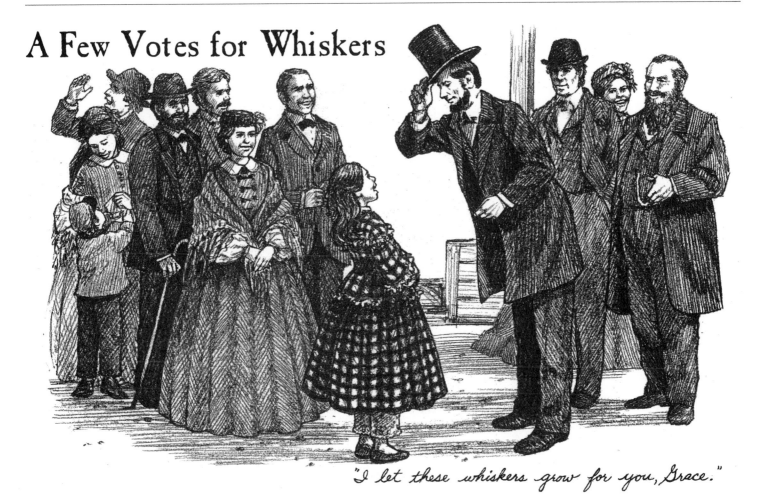

"I let these whiskers grow for you, Grace."

Grace Bedell's father traveled to Illinois in the fall of 1860. He brought home a picture of Abraham Lincoln. Grace decided to write to Mr. Lincoln. This is part of the letter she wrote:

"Dear Sir,

. . . I am a little girl only eleven years old, but want you should be President of the United States very much so I hope you won't think me very bold to write to such a great man as you are. Have you any little girls about as large as I am if so give them my love and tell her to write to me if you cannot answer this letter. I have got four brothers and part of them will vote for you any way and if you will let your whiskers grow I will try and get the rest of them to vote for you you would look a great deal better for your face is so thin. All the ladies like whiskers and they would tease their husbands to vote for you and then you would be President. My father is a going to vote for you and if I was a man I would vote for you. . . . I must not write any more answer this letter right off. Good-bye, Grace Bedell"

Some people were unkind, making fun of Lincoln for the way he dressed. He was very tall and thin, and he complained that it was hard to find clothes that fit well. "Billy the Barber" was in charge of shaving him and trimming his wavy brown hair.

Billy was William Florville, a free black man from Haiti who owned a farm and lots in Springfield, Illinois, Lincoln's hometown. Florville trimmed Lincoln's hair for more than twenty years. He also wrote humorous essays for the newspaper.

After the election, in the weeks before the Lincolns moved to Washington, people began noticing that "Abe" was growing whiskers. One day Billy shaved off Lincoln's

Not Forgotten After All

The Lincoln-Douglas debates, as they were called, drew attention to the lawyer from Springfield. Lincoln sounded like the leader that people in the North had been waiting for. In the South, his name drew scorn. Mary Todd Lincoln's family was from the South, and Lincoln himself was born in Kentucky, a slave state. Lincoln, Southerners cried, had turned against his own roots. Those roots, however, helped him understand and speak kindly of the South, as most Northerners could not.

Lincoln agreed to run for president as a Republican. He won the election for many reasons. He was a "new face" to most Americans. The debates had shown that he was a powerful speaker, a serious thinker, and a compassionate man.

mustache and left a patch of hair on his chin. By the time Lincoln left town, he had a full beard. No one seemed to know why. It was a daring thing for a future president to do.

When Lincoln arrived in Grace Bedell's hometown of Westfield, New York, one of the stops along his wide loop into the nation's capital, he asked if Grace happened to be there. A boy pointed out a blushing young girl in the crowd. Lincoln left his train and made his way over to her. "You see," he told her, smiling, "I let these whiskers grow for you, Grace." He kissed her then, and made headlines in newspapers from New York to Missouri.

THE NOT SO UNITED STATES

Southerners were uneasy about the election of 1860. No southern state voted for Lincoln to be president. To Southerners, Lincoln was a northern president who wanted to stop the expansion of slavery.

South Carolina had had enough. Delegates were chosen, and a secession convention was organized. On December 20, 1860, all 169 delegates voted to secede from, or leave, the United States. Bells rang out all over Charleston, the capital, marking this historic event.

South Carolinians, however, knew that the federal government could easily overwhelm one state. Representatives quickly traveled to other southern states. By February 1861, Mississippi, Florida, Alabama, Georgia, Louisiana, and Texas also seceded from the Union. All of these were slave states.

It was a painful decision to leave the United States and form a southern nation. Most Southern-

ers were loyal to America—this young nation, or Union. They wanted to believe that Lincoln would protect slavery so the Union could be saved.

Lucy Fletcher of Virginia said, "Six of the southern states have followed South Carolina.... There is intense excitement.... Some are for secession, but the majority are opposed to it ... and are willing to remain [in the Union] so long as there is a shadow of hope that our rights will be respected."

"WE MUST NOT BE ENEMIES"

When Abraham Lincoln took the oath of office, he knew that his biggest task was to try and resolve the slavery crisis. The nation could not live as half slave and half free, he said. It would have to become *all* one or the other. In one of his first speeches, he made his feelings clear: "We are not enemies, but friends. We must not be enemies. Though passion may have strained, it must not break our bonds of affection. The mystic chords of memory, stretching from every battlefield and patriot grave to every living heart and hearthstone all over this broad land, will yet swell the chorus of the Union when again touched, as surely they will be, by the better angels of our nature."

L IS FOR LINCOLN

After you design this letter page of your alphabet, think about this: If you could talk to Abraham Lincoln, what three questions would you ask him? Write your three questions on this page of your alphabet book, and then think about them. If you were to answer them, what would you say?

A Nation Divided, 1861

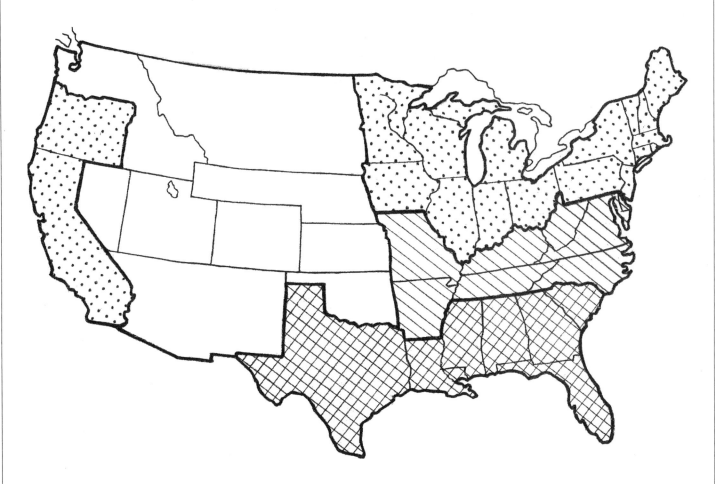

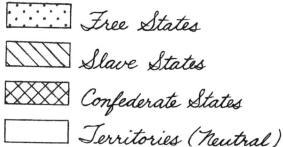

Free States

Slave States

Confederate States

Territories (Neutral)

In the months before the Civil War began, the United States had shattered into two separate nations. This map shows what happened. Of the thirty-three states that existed in April 1861, seven left the Union and created the Confederate States of America (CSA). Four others soon joined them. The rest stuck with the Union. But in four of the states that did (Delaware, Maryland, Kentucky, and Missouri), the people were torn between North and South.

This portrait of Private Edwin Francis Jemison, 2nd Louisiana Regiment, C.S.A., was taken between 1860 and 1862.

WHY JOHN NEEDED TWENTY DOLLARS

John Steele Henderson was fourteen when he wrote home from boarding school in Melville, North Carolina, to ask his parents for money. In the spring of 1861, even schoolboys in the South caught secession fever.

"April 21, 1861

We have had great times here. One Friday night, about thirty five boys, I among them, determined to hoist a secession flag. We had just got it raised, when the enemy [Mr. Wilson, a teacher] came upon us and ordered us to disperse. At first [we] fell back a little, but gathering courage [we] made a bold stand to see what the enemy would do. [Mr. Wilson] tried hard to pull down the flag, but he could not do it. . . . The next morning the flag of the Confederate States was waving over Melville and is waving still. . . . The boys here are going to raise a volunteer company and offer their services to Governor Ellis. I intend to join it and go and help to drive the Abolitionists from the soil of the South, unless my Dear Parents you are unwilling for your son to help fight the battles of his country. If I go may your blessings go with me. O' please let me join! . . . Every boy in school is in favor of secession now and forever. During these times it is hard to study. I think all colleges and schools ought to suspend, until the war is over. O' please don't refuse to let me join this volunteer company! I can't stand here idle, when my country needs my services. I want to fight for my country and if needs be shed the last drop of blood that flows in my veins. I know, it would grieve you to see me leave you and go to war, but I think that you would be proud to see me fighting in the ranks for the rights of the south. If you are willing for me to join please send me about twenty dollars to buy a uniform and other necessary things. . . . May God bless you my Parents and give you fortitude in these troublesome times. My heart is too full to write more.
Your Dutiful and Repentant Son
John"

AN ACT OF WAR

President Lincoln didn't want war. He wanted the United States of America to remain united. Lincoln was willing to allow slavery to continue in slave states if this stopped the nation from being ripped apart. But was Lincoln willing to let the South take Fort Sumter to avoid war? He had to act. The nation was impatient. Newspaper headlines exclaimed, "Have we a government?"

President Lincoln agonized over what to do. He had many sleepless nights. One morning he got out of bed and fainted from nervous exhaustion.

Finally, President Lincoln wrote President Davis a letter stating that he was sending supplies to Fort Sumter. Lincoln was testing Davis. If Davis fired on the supply ships, then it would be the Confederacy that started the war, not him.

As president of the Confederacy, Jefferson Davis had to act as well. He had to be bold or risk having Southerners lose faith in the secession. This could lead to the collapse of the Confederate States of America. President Davis ordered Confederate general P. G. T. Beauregard to take Fort Sumter.

O IS FOR OPINIONS

The South was leaving the Union. The *New York Tribune* newspaper said, "There's the door—go!"

Frederick Douglass was a runaway slave whose education and wisdom had made him famous in the North. Douglass traveled throughout the North, speaking out against slavery. When he heard of the southern secession, he said, "If the Union can only be maintained by new concessions [compromises] to the slaveholders [and] a new drain on the Negro's blood . . . let the Union perish."

In May of 1861, Great Britain declared the South to be an "organized military power" but wouldn't accept the Confederate States of America as a true nation. President Lincoln felt the secession of the South was simply an unlawful act. The Constitution of the United States didn't grant states the right to leave the Union.

The Civil War Begins

A blast lit the night sky. The ground shook. Windows rattled. Children and parents jumped out of bed. Another blast! Families left their Charleston homes, gathering at the docks. There, along the shoreline, they saw southern artillerists firing on Fort Sumter, located on an island in the harbor.

The day had finally come. For too long, the people of Charleston had watched a U.S. flag fly over Fort Sumter. The fort was in a Confederate harbor. It was going to belong to the Confederacy.

Mary Boykin Chesnut, who lived in Charleston, wrote, "I prayed as I never prayed before. . . . The shells were bursting. . . . The regular roar of the cannon—there it was. . . . The women were wild there on the housetops . . . and everybody wondered that Fort Sumter did not fire a shot."

Inside Fort Sumter, for the moment, the 128 military men and civilians were safe. The walls, made of brick and concrete, were forty feet high and twelve feet thick. The fort's 110 guns were among the biggest the Union army had ever made.

As day broke, Major Anderson, the commander of the fort, and the other residents sat down to a breakfast of pork and water. The mood was calm. But Major Anderson was worried. Food supplies were desperately low. In two days all the food would be gone. Major Anderson hoped Union reinforcements would come to their rescue.

What Is a Government?

President Jefferson Davis believed America was founded on the idea that a government is genuine only if it supports the beliefs of the people. The U.S. government didn't support the expansion of slavery. The South did. Therefore, the U.S. government wasn't lawful. Southerners had no choice but to create a new nation that supported slavery.

After breakfast, Union gunners took their positions. They fired their guns across the harbor at the Confederate positions. Around them, enemy shells smashed into upper sections of the fort walls, filling the air with smoke and dust.

By day's end, Major Anderson still had no reinforcements. With only seventy-nine military men at his disposal, he decided to forbid his artillerists from using the fort's biggest guns, atop the fort's wall. These positions were extremely vulnerable to enemy fire. Major Anderson could not afford to lose the few men he had.

The next day Confederate gunners fired without mercy at Fort Sumter. Union men gallantly fired back from more protected positions, but they were outmatched. Shells smashed into the fort's wooden barracks. The structure burst into flames. A westerly wind fanned the fire. Men doused blankets in water and covered cannon shells to prevent them from exploding.

Soldiers and civilians choked as they tried to breathe the oven-hot air, thick with smoke. Men covered their faces with wet rags to avoid being scalded. Others lay down on the earthen floor, hoping to find breathable air.

Men covered their faces to avoid being scalded.

A Deadly Celebration

Four thousand rounds of ammunition were fired at Fort Sumter, and not one Confederate or Union soldier died.

But during the celebration the next day, one of Fort Sumter's big guns was fired by rebel soldiers. Burning fragments fell and ignited a pile of cartridges. The cartridges exploded, killing Confederate artillerist Private Daniel Hough. Five other soldiers were wounded. One man died several days later. Private Hough was buried in Fort Sumter.

High above the fort, the U.S. flag flew, wavered, then fell. A chorus of loud cheers came from southern spectators watching on nearby islands and the mainland. Union men had withstood the Confederate attack for thirty-four hours. They had survived 4,000 rounds of ammunition. They could withstand no more. Major Anderson surrendered.

The news caused Southerners to be overcome with joy. In Richmond, Virginia, a crowd fired off a cannon in front of the capitol. In North Carolina, women threw bunches of flowers onto the streets below as men gave each other hearty slaps and cheered for Jefferson Davis and the Confederacy. A journalist from the *London Times* reported seeing "flushed faces, wild eyes, screaming mouths."

There was no turning back. The Civil War had begun.

The 50¢ note of 1864 had a picture of President Jefferson Davis on it.

Jefferson Davis was the first and only president of the Confederate States of America. Many Confederate congressmen called him "Majesty Davis" because he preferred to rule rather than guide the Confederate government. Confederate congressmen had their faults, too. They made no attempt to build agreement among their states or even one another. Fights broke out in the Congress, and congressmen rarely came to work on a regular basis.

MONEY TALKS

Turn over a dollar bill. Have you ever noticed the pyramid and the eye glowing in a triangle above it? Have you noticed that the eagle is holding a shield or the Latin words *E Pluribus Unum* around the eagle's head?

The United States government chose these symbols to tell the world what we thought about ourselves and our nation. The pyramid, with its thirteen rows representing the thirteen colonies, was chosen to stand for strength and duration. The fact that the pyramid is unfinished means that our job as a nation is not finished; there is progress to be made. The eye stands for the eye of providence, or judgment, that always watches over us. The eagle stands for power and victory. The shield represents self-reliance. The words *E Pluribus Unum* means out of many [states] one [nation].

When the Confederate States of America was created, the new government had to create a new currency. The 50¢ note had a picture of President Jefferson Davis to honor the Confederate president. The $500 note was adorned with symbols of war: the Confederate battle flag, the drum and bugle, the backside of three cannons, a soldier on a horse, and the picture of General "Stonewall" Jackson.

Making Money

If you had the power to create an imaginary currency, what would your paper money look like? What color would it be? What words would appear on your money, and what language would the words come from? Would you choose symbols that tell something about the nation? Would you choose symbols that tell what you believe money stands for? Is money all-powerful? Is it something to be used to make the world better?

You Will Need:

Graphite and colored pencils; pens; paints; drawing paper; possibly construction paper; an encyclopedia or other resource books.

1. Take a look at various countries' currencies. An encyclopedia is a good resource.

2. Sketch a design for your currency on drawing paper. You may want to photocopy pictures of various currencies and create a collage of known currency symbols and your own original symbols.

3. You may want to use colored pencils or paints— or a combination of various mediums. It's your money!

P IS FOR PRESERVATION

When South Carolina seceded from the United States, the Upper South states (North Carolina, Tennessee, Virginia, and Arkansas) issued a warning to the federal government: if you try to force the seven seceded states back into the Union, we will also secede.

When Southerners risked their lives to capture Fort Sumter, the Upper South states realized that issuing another warning would be too weak a response. Instead, they joined the Confederacy. Even though only 20 percent of white families in the South owned slaves, all Southerners realized that being white in a slave society allowed *all* whites, whether they owned slaves or not, to be superior to blacks. Many believed this superiority was worth fighting for.

THE CONFEDERATE STATES OF AMERICA

In Montgomery, Alabama, the capital of this new southern nation, President Jefferson Davis and a growing number of people set about creating a new government. Unfortunately, Montgomery, for all its good will, was too small to house the expanding Confederate government.

President Davis set up his office in a hotel parlor because there wasn't enough room in the capitol for his office. Other government workers lived in crowded, filthy rooms. They had no cooks, house-keepers, or even beds. They slept on the floor and ate such food as "unknown" fish, possums, and frogs, served on dirty plates.

After four months in Montgomery, the Confederate capital moved to Richmond, Virginia—just 100 miles from Washington, D.C. Richmond had the largest industrial center in the South, access to water transportation by the James River and the Atlantic Ocean, and five railroads that served the city. The city of Richmond was also close to the North—where the South hoped, *if war came*, most of the fighting would take place.

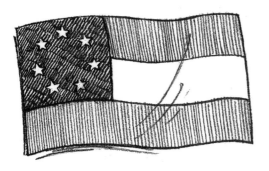

THE "STARS AND BARS"

The "Stars and Bars" Confederate flag was used for more than two years, but it was never established as the official Confederate flag. Many people liked the "Stars and Bars" because it reminded them of the U.S. flag.

THE "STAINLESS BANNER"

The "Stainless Banner" was the flag of the Confederacy from May 1, 1863, to March 4, 1865. Many Southerners felt the flag's large white section made it look like a flag of surrender. On March 4, 1865, a red stripe was added to reduce the flag's white color.

Just as many children today stand and pledge allegiance to the flag in school, each morning Confederate children also pledged their allegiance to the Confederate flag. Here is what they said: *I salute the Confederate flag with affection, reverence, and undying devotion to the Cause for which it stands.*

THE BATTLE FLAG

William Miles's design, submitted in 1861, became the battle flag of the Confederate armies. Today it's the most widely recognized of all the Confederate flags. The seven stars represent the seven original southern states to secede from the Union. Later versions of this flag displayed thirteen stars. The twelfth and thirteenth stars stood for two rebel state governments located in the Union states of Missouri and Kentucky.

A WHOLLY ORIGINAL FLAG

As time passed, more people were tiring of the "Stars and Bars." They wanted a Confederate flag that looked nothing like the United States flag. In 1862 a totally new flag design was created. The sun in the flag's center represented the Confederacy's generosity, security, and supremacy. This flag design was never accepted.

Louis Crenshaw's Flag

Louis D. Crenshaw Jr., a fifteen-year-old boy of Richmond, Virginia, had a plan. It was the spring of 1861, and everyone was caught up in secession fever. Soon Virginia was sure to leave the Union. Louis Crenshaw was too impatient to wait. He gathered his sisters and made a Confederate flag out of red, white, and blue flannel. When the flag was finished, he raised it up a homemade flagpole. It was the first Confederate flag ever raised.

The Crenshaws' flag was just the start of a parade of various Confederate flag creations. The Confederate Congress established a committee to find a design for a Confederate flag by March 4, 1861—the date President Lincoln would be inaugurated as the Union president. Many flag designs were submitted. The "Stars and Bars" design was chosen. But the design would be changed several times during the war.

The Battle at Bull Run: A Play

CAST OF CHARACTERS

Narrator
Girl #1
Sister
Father
Senator Wilson
Jennie
Lost Union Soldier
Rosie O'Neal Greenhow
Betty Duvall
Confederate Soldiers #1 & 2
General M. L. Bonham
Northern Reporters #1–7
Southern Reporters #1–4
General Irvin McDowell
Confederate General
    Pierce G. T. Beauregard
"Fresh Fish" Union Soldier
Reserve Union Soldiers
Rebel Soldiers
General Daniel Tyler
Anxious Union Soldier
Confederate Colonel
    Nathan Evans
Woman in Cabin
Union Soldier in Awe
Judith Henry
Confederate Captain
Confederate General
    Joseph E. Johnston
Confederate Colonel
    Francis S. Bartow
Confederate General
    Bernard Bee
Confederate General
    "Stonewall" Jackson
Union Officers
Veteran Soldier
President Jefferson Davis

STAGING SUGGESTIONS

All Union troops can enter from the left. All Confederate troops can enter from the right. To facilitate the staging, divide all Confederate and Union troops into "regiments" under the various Union and rebel officers.

Center stage can be the hill where Judith Henry's farm is located. The center can also be used, at other times, to stage such action as the Confederate captain using signal flags. Upstage center can be a wooded area where Confederate soldiers fire on General Tyler. This staging, of course, can be altered. The staging of specific scenes will depend on your performance space. Remember, keep the action simple. Troops, for example, can march in place to give the illusion of forward motion. Officers on horses can be mimed.

SCENE 1

Narrator: July 21, 1861. A hot Sunday morning on the banks between Bull Run and Cub Run in Virginia. From Washington, approximately twenty miles away, spectators arrive to see the first major battle of the Civil War.

Girl #1 *(holding a picnic basket)*: This is just lovely, isn't it, Sister?

Sister *(looking for a place to put down her blanket)*: Father, where's the best place to view the battle?

Father *(wiping his brow)*: Wherever we sit, we will roast. Good morning, Senator Wilson. You have come to see our boys end this war today?

Senator Wilson *(approaches, eating a sweet)*: Yes, and the boys in blue from my Massachusetts will lead the victory, though I'm sure the others here may disagree.

COSTUME SUGGESTIONS

Union soldiers: dark blue shirts and light blue pants

Confederate soldiers: light gray shirts and sky-blue pants

Girls: cotton dresses

Reporters: straw hats with signs saying *Confederate reporter* or *Union reporter*

Officers: Stetson-style hats (Check secondhand stores.)

PROP SUGGESTIONS

Guns: one arm extended and held stiff

Gunfire sound: popping bubble wrap or a wooden "slapstick"

Wigwag signal flags: check an encyclopedia for details. The flags can be made out of dowels and paper.

Picnic baskets and the material for the envelope: check secondhand stores.

Girl #1 *(calling out into the crowd)*: Jennie, Jennie! Is that you? *(Jennie comes over, leaving her family. The girls giggle.)* Is that a new dress? It's as bright as the summer sun.

Jennie: I got it especially for today. Isn't this too glorious? Finally, a new war! I won't have to listen to Father's stories of 1812 and the Mexican War ever again. *(A New York soldier ENTERS, wearing a fancy "Zouave" uniform of baggy red knickers, purple blouse, a short blue jacket with a big sash, and red fez hat. He's lost.)*

Girl #1: Look! A soldier!

Sister: A real soldier!

Jennie: I'm going to faint! *(They gather around the embarrassed young man. Jennie leads the way.)*

Jennie: What are you doing here?

Lost Soldier: I got lost from my regiment, the New York Zouaves. *(The girls giggle.)* There were thousands of soldiers gathered in Washington, miss. It was dizzying.

Jennie: But none as dashing as you in your uniform.

Lost Soldier *(proudly)*: It's just like the uniform of the incredible light infantry troops of Algeria, I think.

Girl #1, Jennie, and Sister: Algeria!

Girl #1: Sit with us, please.

Lost Soldier: I should be trying to find my regiment.

Jennie: Just for a minute.

Sister: Tell me, is it true, spies are everywhere?

Lost Soldier: I cannot say, miss, for sure.

Girl #1: Perhaps you are a spy disguised as a soldier? *(They all laugh. Laughter fades. Actors EXIT.)*

One Battle, Two Names

Throughout the Civil War, the South and the North often gave different names to the same battle. The Union named battles after landmarks such as creeks or hills where fighting took place. They called the first major battle the Battle at Bull Run, after the creek of that name.

The Confederacy named battles after the town serving as their base of military operations. Since their base for the first battle was in Manassas, the South called the first major conflict of the Civil War the Battle at Manassas.

The Glory of War

Rebel and Yankee soldiers were eager for the war to start. They believed it would be glorious. One New York volunteer wrote home after he enlisted, "I and the rest of the boys are in fine spirits . . . feeling like larks." In the South, one rebel soldier from Arkansas wrote, "So impatient did I become for starting that I felt like ten thousand pins were pricking me in every part of the body, and started off a week in advance of my brother."

SCENE 2

Narrator: Eleven days before the Battle at Bull Run. July 10, 1861, Washington, D.C., at the home of Confederate spy Rosie O'Neal Greenhow, a wealthy southern widow. No secret can be hidden from Rosie—not even the Union's most closely guarded news: when the Union soldiers will leave Washington to do battle at Bull Run. (*As the Narrator speaks, Rosie finishes writing a coded message, folds it, and sews it into a silk envelope. Beside her, Betty Duvall gets into a farm girl disguise. Narrator EXITS.*)

Rosie (*looking at Betty*)**:** Remove your necklace, Betty. You are a farm girl.

Betty (*nervously*)**:** I forgot I had it on.

Rosie: There's nothing to worry about. (*Rosie gathers Betty's long hair, ties the silk envelope inside it, and arranges Betty's hair into a knot at the top of her head—holding it in place with a "tucking comb."*) There. You are ready. You know what to do?

Betty: Yes. Drive the vegetable cart out of Washington. Spend the night at the family of Lieutenant Jones. The next day, change into riding clothes and go on horseback to the Confederate line at Fairfax Courthouse. How did you get the information, anyway? Was it from that Senator Wilson who admires you so?

Rosie: Get on your way. (*Actors EXIT.*)

SCENE 3

Narrator: The next day near Fairfax Courthouse. (*Narrator EXITS.*)

Confederate Soldier #1: I told you General Bonham's orders are that no more women are to be let through. You could be a Yankee spy.

Betty (*frustrated*)**:** I must see General Bonham immediately. I have vital information. Send me away, and you'll regret your decision for the rest of your life. (*The soldier takes Betty to General Bonham's headquarters. She is escorted before the General.*)

Betty (*to General Bonham*)**:** I have important information for General Beauregard. Can you forward it to him or may I, with your permission, take it to him myself?

General Bonham: I will have it forwarded at once. (*Betty lets down her long hair, unties the package, and hands it to the general. (They freeze as Narrator ENTERS.*)

Narrator: The message is rushed to General Beauregard at his Manassas headquarters and then taken to President Davis. The message gives the date Union General McDowell's forces will depart Washington for Manassas: "McDowell has certainly been ordered to advance on the sixteenth. R.O.G. [Rosie O'Neal Greenhow]."

Rosie will send two more coded messages before the Battle of Manassas, describing the number of McDowell's troops and a Union plan to cut the rail line in order to stop Confederate reinforce-

ments from reaching Manassas. The young men of the Union army know little about spies. They know even less about being soldiers. *(Actors EXIT.)*

SCENE 4

Narrator *(Union soldiers are behind him.)*: July 16, five days before the battle. Union troops approach Fairfax Courthouse. They are waiting. Troops up ahead have stopped to eat berries.

Northern Reporter #1 *(taking notes)*: I am here with Union soldiers—30,000 men, I am told. Their faces are covered in sweat and dust. They have been walking for miles in the heat, squinting each time their guns flash sunlight in their eyes. These soldiers carry fifty-pound packs and are constantly moving fallen trees from the road, cut down by Confederate soldiers to slow the Union troops' advance. The Union men can barely stand up. If their officers had any sense, they'd tell these boys to break ranks and take a nap.

General McDowell *(He rides by, stops, and addresses the audience.)*: This is taking too long and there's nothing I, General McDowell, can do about it. I just received these troops today. Too many of

these men are untrained. Any sudden surprise will surely scare them. Officers, listen! Blundering onto the enemy will not be pardonable in any commander. *(Everyone EXITS.)*

SCENE 5

(In the remaining scenes, northern and southern newspaper reporters are positioned among the action, with their respective sides. They are taking notes, occasionally looking at their pocket watches.)

Northern Reporter #2 *(yawning)*: 2 A.M., July 21. We are at Centerville. The troops have been awake for several hours. Bull Run lies below among scattered patches of oak and pine trees. A bright moon shines as soldiers move up and down, readying six-team horses to carry gun carriages, organizing wagons and ambulances.

"Fresh Fish" [Inexperienced] Union Soldier: It looks like a bristling monster lifting himself by a slow wavy motion. *(General McDowell's Union troops move very slowly as General Tyler's men move upstage toward waiting rebel soldiers.)*

Northern Reporter #3: As soldiers move out, troops being held in reserve cheer the others on.

Reserve Union Soldiers *(shouting repeatedly)*: Get us a souvenir! Get us a traitor's scalp!

A Thimbleful of Blood

President Lincoln's first appeal for Union states to provide 75,000 militiamen for ninety days was based on a belief that the war wouldn't last more than three months.

Senator James Chesnut of South Carolina also believed the war would be over quickly. He offered to drink all the blood shed as a consequence of leaving the Union. Many Southerners declared, "A lady's thimble will hold all the blood that will be shed."

In the Battle at Bull Run, more than 625 Union soldiers were killed and mortally wounded, 950 soldiers were injured, and 1,200 were captured. On the Confederate side, 400 men were killed, 1,600 were wounded, and 225 men would later die of their wounds.

A Deadly Mix-Up

During the Battle at Bull Run, Confederate and Union soldiers mainly wore gray or blue uniforms, but they were of many different styles. This hodgepodge of Union and Confederate uniforms made it difficult to know which soldiers were the enemy on the battlefield.

During the Battle at Bull Run, Union cannons were firing into the Confederate column. Union firepower was overwhelming the enemy. From the distance came a regiment dressed in blue. Thinking they were Union troops sent to assist them, the northern artillerists stopped firing. The troops in blue turned out to be Confederate soldiers, who attacked the Union gunners and wiped them out.

SCENE 6

Northern Reporter #4: 5:30 A.M. General Daniel Tyler's four Union regiments, along with cavalry and artillery, have reached Bull Run—a two-mile march. Tyler's troops are ahead of McDowell's men. Their pace is torturously slow. The sun appears, exposing patches of blackberry bushes in the valley. Soldiers wander off to have an early-morning snack.

Northern Reporter #5: There are trees before us. We can see the reflection of the enemy's bayonets in the woods. Three companies are sent into the woods. General Tyler orders a great thirty-two-pound Parrot gun to be fired at the Confederate enemy. The echo is tremendous. The hills shake. I am shaking. Bright light appears from the trees as the shells explode. From the woods, rebels fire at us. We cannot see them. No one knows where they are. *(Several Union soldiers fall.)*

Rebel Soldiers *(hidden, screaming)*: Now, you Yankee devils, we've got you where we want you!

Anxious Union Soldier *(out loud to himself)*: Why don't they come out and fight? *(then to the rebels)* I'll fight three times your number out in the open field!

Northern Reporter #6: We continue firing our big guns until the rebels are quiet, but General Tyler will not go after them. He is satisfied simply to have silenced them. *(A Confederate captain ENTERS and wigwags, or uses signal flags, to convey where the enemy is.)*

Confederate Colonel Evans *(positioned farther downstage, receives and relays signals to headquarters with flags)*: Let's meet the enemy. *(He moves his troops to right of center stage. All other Confederate officers except General Beauregard move their troops as well.)*

Confederate General Beauregard *(with his troops downstage, to the far right of the enemy)*: My rebel soldiers, I have received word that Union troops are not concentrated here at the railroad junction. They are to the north. I don't believe this message. We will remain here.

Narrator: While Confederate General Beauregard remains at the railroad junction, Confederate troops fire on Union General McDowell's approaching army of 10,000.

Southern Reporter #1: The Union boys are coming. Fortunately for us, the regiments don't fire on the rebels all at once. They look tired.

Woman in Cabin *(leaning out of her doorway)*: There are enough Confederates up ahead, including my husband, to whip the lot of you Yanks.

Union Soldier in Awe: Bullets are flying past me. What a strange noise they make. *(He falls down dead.)*

SCENE 7

(Spectators watching the battle.)
Girl #1: This is boring.
Sister: All I see is smoke.
Jennie: Want some lemonade?
Senator Wilson: I do.
Lost Soldier: It all looks so confusing.

SCENE 8

(Judith Henry ENTERS. She's positioned above, in the center, as rebel troops, from the right, and Union troops, from the left, converge on her hillside farm.)
Northern Reporter #7: Near 12 noon. McDowell's forces and Tyler have met. Rebels are retreating.
Judith Henry *(the sounds of cannon and gunfire are heard)*: I am Judith Henry. I am eighty-four years old. This is my farmhouse. Here I lie, too sick to leave my bed. Here I lie, listening to the sound of bullets and shells shattering the walls of my home, and I can do nothing about it.
Southern Reporter #2: It's 4 P.M. and Confederate General Johnston has just come by train from the Shenandoah Valley with fresh troops. *(Johnston ENTERS, stage right, with Confederate troops.)*
Confederate General Johnston: The battle is over there—I am going. *(Johnston and his men join other Confederate forces on stage.)*

Southern Reporter #3: Colonel Evans's rebels are dog tired. More Confederate forces, under the command of Confederate General Bee, are moving back downhill.
Confederate Colonel Bartow *(holding a Confederate flag)*: General Beauregard says you must hold this position, Georgians. I appeal to you to hold on! *(A shot kills him.)*
Confederate General Bee *(riding over to General Stonewall Jackson on the hill)*: General, they are beating us back.
Confederate General Jackson: Sir, we will give them the bayonet. *(Jackson, on horseback, takes his men forward. General Bee goes off to show his troops Jackson's heroic stance.)*
Confederate General Bee *(shouting)*: Look! There is Jackson, standing like a stone wall! Rally behind the Virginians! *(Bee falls from his horse dead. Union and rebel soldiers fight on Henry Hill. An explosion is heard. Judith Henry slumps to her side and dies.)*
Southern Reporter #4: For one long mile the whole valley is a boiling crater of dust and smoke.
Narrator: And into the smoke and gunfire, General Beauregard finally arrives to join Confederate reinforcements on horseback. Union soldiers are bewildered and frightened. Their common urge is to run for cover. Young men fall dead with blackberry-stained lips. *(General Jackson, injured, crosses downstage right to be treated.)*

Caring for the Enemy

Some Confederate and Union soldiers risked their lives helping wounded enemy soldiers because they saw these men as fellow Americans in need of help.

President Davis wrote to his wife about witnessing such an act of kindness. "In riding over the field of Manassas, I encountered a Federal soldier of whom it was said that, although he might have retreated in safety with the Federal army, he had remained within our line to nurse a wounded Confederate officer. . . . I ordered that in consideration of his humanity he should not be treated as a prisoner of war."

Various Union Officers: Don't run. Line up! Don't run!

Veteran Soldier: Look at the young ones run. They do not know they are safer here, staying in our ranks.

Southern Reporters: We are winning!

Northern Reporters: All is lost!

President Davis (entering stage right, out of breath): I have come from Richmond, eighty miles by train and then by horse. (Davis sees dejected, wounded rebel soldiers who left the battle before seeing the rebel victory.)

Confederate Soldier #2: Go back! We are whipped!

President Davis: I am President Davis! Follow me back to the field! (Then to himself) Is this to be our beginning and our end?

Confederate General Jackson (his wounds being treated; to Davis): We have whipped them! They ran like sheep! Give me 5,000 fresh men and I will be in Washington City tomorrow!

SCENE 9

Girl #1: Why are all those soldiers coming toward us?

Father (fearful): Quick, my daughters, we must leave! (The spectators are overrun by retreating soldiers. Spectators become terrified participants. Spectators scream. Union soldiers and spectators EXIT, leaving dead Union and rebel soldiers onstage. Victorious rebel soldiers surround President Jefferson Davis. They lift him up.)

WE ARE BEATEN, WHIPPED

Many Northerners were shocked and humiliated over the defeat at Bull Run. A Northerner who was overwhelmed by the battle's outcome proclaimed the day after the Sunday battle as "Black Monday." He wrote further, "We are utterly and disgracefully routed, beaten, whipped." Horace Greeley wrote in his *New York Tribune*, "If it is best for the country and for mankind that we make peace with the rebels, and on their own terms, do not shrink even from that."

In contrast, southern newspapers and politicians were puffed up with pride over the Confederate's first victory. Thomas R. R. Cobb, a politician from Georgia, stated that the victory at Manassas "has secured our independence."

Other Southerners were more cautious. They believed the victory would make the Confederacy overly confident and wake up the North's determination to win.

President Lincoln wasn't paralyzed by the defeat. The Battle at Bull Run was the first, not the last, battle of the war. Lincoln put the defeat behind him and focused on creating a successful war strategy. A day after the Bull Run defeat, Lincoln signed a bill asking for 500,000 soldiers to be enlisted for three years—not three months.

President Lincoln had trouble finding a strong leader for the Union army. He wanted Robert E. Lee, a Virginian, to lead it, but Lee refused. As much as he loved the Union, he would not fight against the people of his own state. The North's greatest military leader, Winfield Scott, was too old for battle, but he helped the president plan war strategy. He finally agreed to serve until November 1862. After trying several other generals, Lincoln gave the highest command to Ulysses S. Grant.

Not So Glorious

After the Union defeat at Bull Run, Union soldier Charles Putnam wrote a letter to his brother George on July 26, 1861:

"I tell you what it is, George, that was the hardest day's work I ever did. We started at 2 o'clock in the morning, marched eighteen miles, and right on the battlefield without any rest or breakfast, and many of the men had no water in their canteens. . . . It was an awful sight to see such brave men slaughtered as they were, and what looked almost as bad, to see the noble horses cut to pieces by the cannon balls. . . . During thirty-six hours we marched over sixty miles, besides being on the field seven hours, with nothing to eat but hard bread, and nothing to drink but muddy water."

Glory Gone

Thirteen months after Bull Run, the glory of war was still missing. A Georgian soldier who fought at Gaines's Mill, near Richmond, wrote, "I felt quite small in that fight the other day when the musket balls and cannon balls was flying around me as thick as hail and my best friends falling on both sides dead and mortally wounded. Oh Dear, it is impossible for me to express my feelings when the fight was over & saw what was done the tears came then free oh that I never could behold such a sight again to think of it among civilized people killing one another like beasts."

FREEMEN!
AVOID CONSCRIPTION!

The undersigned desires to raise a Company for the Confederate States service, and for that purpose I call upon the people of the Counties of Jefferson and Hawkins, Tenn., to meet promptly at Russellville, on SATURDAY, JULY 19th, 1862, and organize a Company.

By so doing you will avoid being taken as Conscripts, for that Act will now be enforced by order of the War Department. Rally, then, my Countrymen, to your Country's call.

S. M. DENNISON,
Of the Confederate States Army.

CHARLESTON, Tenn., JUNE 30, 1862.

This advertisement called for Tennessee men to form their own Confederate company rather than face the shame of being ordered by the government to join the army.

BROTHERS ON THE BATTLEFIELD

When the war began, soldiers on each side believed their army would have a quick victory and march home as heroes. Colonel William Tecumseh Sherman knew otherwise. He lined up his young recruits on the parade field.

"There are a lot of boys here who believe that war is all glory," he began. "I am telling those boys now that they are wrong. . . . War is Hell!" The young soldiers didn't want to hear his message, and they didn't believe it.

From North to South, hundreds of thousands of young men lined up in regiments, ready for battle. We have no numbers, but most of the boys who fought in the war were younger than twenty-one. Many fought beside their own brothers. The five Newhall brothers, for example, enlisted in a Massachusetts regiment in October 1861. One was killed at Bull Run, and one was captured. Two were sharpshooters who fought together under General Grant. When the fifth brother was badly wounded, his father wrote to President Lincoln, asking if the boy could return home. Lincoln gave his permission.

Boys on the Battlefield

A person had to be eighteen years old to enlist in the Union or Confederate army. That was the law. The law was often ignored.

Some parents gave written consent for their younger sons to join the army. Some boys lied about their age. Enlistment officers persuaded underage boys to enlist, leaving distraught parents to write letters begging their government to find and return their children.

Brother Fought Brother

Sometimes, a brother *was* the enemy. In Massachusetts, for example, five Bixby brothers went to war for the Union. Henry and George were captured by the Confederates. Henry was released and went home. When George was released, he joined the Confederate army. A third brother deserted the Union. The other two brothers, Charles and Oliver, died fighting for the North.

Many families lost most, or all, of their sons. A New York family sent three sons into battle. One was killed on the battlefield, the second died in prison, and the third lay sick in an army hospital. The family wrote to Lincoln, and Lincoln discharged the surviving son.

The Final Toll

The Civil War lasted four years, and when it ended, more than 6 million soldiers were dead, missing, or wounded. In deaths alone, it is still the worst war in United States history. If the totals of American soldiers killed in all other wars are added together, it still does not equal the number who died in the Civil War.

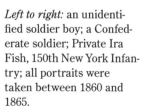
Left to right: an unidentified soldier boy; a Confederate soldier; Private Ira Fish, 150th New York Infantry; all portraits were taken between 1860 and 1865.

Headquarters

53d Reg't N. C. Militia,

Fayetteville, April 18, 1862.

I am authorized by the Adjutant General of the State to purchase

DOUBLE-BARREL SHOT-GUNS and GOOD RIFLES,

for the use of the Militia of Cumberland county. Any persons having Guns of the proper description can get the full value in *Cash*, by passing them in to A. M. Johnson, Quartermaster, or Dr. Theo. Martine, Ordnance Officer of the Regiment. All Officers are requested to disseminate this information and to facilitate the purchase of Arms for the purpose named.

JOHN H. COOK,
Col. Com'dg.

The advertisement at left calls for Southerners to sell their guns to help overcome the Confederacy's terrible shortage of rifles and shotguns. Many Southerners believed that *had* the War department provided the necessary weapons to Confederate troops at the Battle at Bull Run, they could have pursued retreating Union troops back to Washington and possibly ended the war right then.

One reason for the lack of weapons was the fact that individual southern states were hoarding weapons to protect themselves from a possible enemy invasion and the chance of slave uprisings. The *Macon Daily Telegraph* printed a jingle telling rebel soldiers how to increase their supply of guns: "Want a weapon? Why, capture one! / Every Doodle has got a gun, / Belt and bayonet, bright, and new; / Kill a Doodle, and capture two!"

Cannonballs, torpedoes, shot, and shells were stored in arsenal yards.

The Battle of Shiloh

Shiloh National Cemetery

One hundred thousand men fought at Shiloh. It was one of the bloodiest battles of the war; the aftermath was a gruesome scene. Grant wrote that one field was covered in a solid layer of bodies—3,000 lay dead, 20,000 were wounded.

Four years later, Shiloh National Cemetery was established. Sixty-eight hundred soldiers, many of them killed on the fields of Shiloh, lie buried there.

Until April of 1862, only a handful of folks had heard of Shiloh Church, near the banks of the Tennessee River. The little wooden sanctuary sat on rolling land crossed by creeks and dotted with springs and ponds.

On April 5, Union soldiers of General Ulysses S. Grant's army camped beside the river, not far from the church. The soldiers were energized by their capture of Forts Henry and Donelson, in northern Tennessee. They had won the first major victory for the North. Now they waited for General Don Carlos Buell and his Army of the Ohio. United, they would attack the South at Corinth, Mississippi.

But early in the morning of April 6, 1862, rebel soldiers commanded by General Albert S. Johnston attacked, catching Grant off guard. Union troops scrambled to safety along a sunken wagon road. All morning the soldiers fought intensely in a field that was later named the Hornet's Nest. During the afternoon, General Johnston took a bullet

in his leg. Refusing aid, he rested under a tree near his men, where he died of massive bleeding.

Before nightfall, the South, under General Beauregard, finally pushed the Union army back against the river. The death toll was high. Too wounded to move, many soldiers on both sides died trying to get water, giving Bloody Pond its name.

As rain fell, Union soldiers took cover for the night. While they slept, General Buell and General Wallace arrived with 20,000 soldiers. The next day, they outfought the rebels. Facing defeat, Beauregard called for a retreat.

Stunned by his huge loss of men, General Grant could not follow them. When Northerners learned of the high death toll, they placed the blame on Grant. Some critics said his boldness was really incompetence. General Buell took credit for the Union victory and transferred Grant's army to General Henry Halleck.

CIGARS FOR THE ENEMY

In September of 1862, Union and rebel armies made their camps near the village of Sharpsburg, Maryland, along Antietam [an-TEE-tum] Creek. General George McClellan, head of the Union soldiers, ordered his men to chase the rebels from the creek. Walking near the battlefield, a Union private spotted some cigars wrapped in paper on the ground. Unwrapping them, he saw that the paper contained military notes. The private passed the paper to his superior officers, who delivered it to General McClellan. The general studied it with great interest. It contained Robert E. Lee's strategy for dividing his army and attacking the North.

General Lee, tall, gray-haired, brown-eyed, and handsome, had just taken command of the Army of Northern Virginia. His men were celebrating. They had captured Union weapons that were stored at the supply base at Manassas Junction, Virginia. Fifty-two thousand rebels had forced General John Pope's Union soldiers to retreat toward Washington.

It was harvesttime in the cornfields. Lee wanted to protect the crop and strike a victory on northern soil. His soldiers waded across the sandy Potomac River, singing "Dixie" as they reached the Maryland shore.

But thanks to Lee's "cigar" notes, General McClellan and his 87,000 men were ready. On September 17, the armies clashed in the bloodiest battle in American history. They fought north of Sharpsburg, in cornfields owned by Union farmers. By evening, 4,000 dead bodies covered the fields and nearly 22,000 were wounded. Many of those would not survive.

Lee's defeated rebel army straggled back across the Potomac, and the Union army, as at Shiloh, was again too stunned to follow and fight. After the battle, many Northerners thought that McClellan might have ended the war if he had captured Lee as the rebels departed.

With big losses on their side, too, the North could not call this a true victory. But it marked a turning point in the Civil War. General Lee wanted a southern victory to bring help from Britain and France. But Queen Victoria and Napoleon Bonaparte now wondered if the South could win the war.

In the North, a profound event followed. President Lincoln called a meeting of his advisers. As they listened to his lighthearted opening remarks, they could not guess what would follow. After removing his eyeglasses, the president announced his plan to emancipate, or free, the slaves.

Dead Confederate soldiers were hastily buried in a ditch. Antietam, Maryland, 1862.

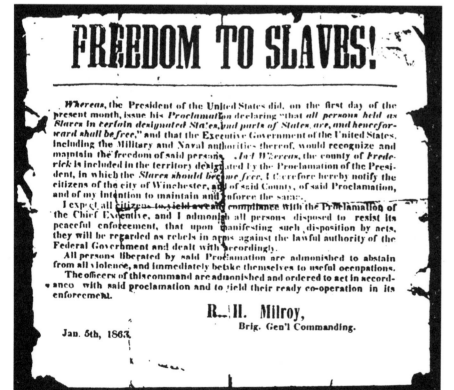

A broadside warns the citizens of Winchester, Virginia, to obey President Lincoln's order to free the slaves.

EMANCIPATION

Before Lincoln became president, he promised that slavery would be accepted where it already existed, but that it could not spread farther. In the summer of 1862, he changed his mind.

After the Battle of Antietam, Lincoln announced the Emancipation Proclamation. Under certain conditions, it granted freedom to slaves. President Lincoln used his special wartime powers to enact the proclamation without the approval of Congress. He believed it would help end the war and save the Union.

The Emancipation Proclamation took effect when President Lincoln signed it on January 1, 1863. When the order went into effect, Henry Turner, a black minister in Washington, D.C., ran to the newspaper office. The Emancipation Proclamation was rolling off the press. Pushing through the crowd, Turner grabbed for a copy of Lincoln's order freeing the slaves.

Waving the paper in his hand, Turner was surrounded by excited people. They burst into cheers and raised him onto a platform. Breathless from running, he began to read. In the street, people shouted with glee, shook hands, and sang songs. A cannon began booming.

The order gave freedom to every slave whose owner was in rebellion against the North, and it allowed former slaves to enlist in the Union army. Black men and boys in the North, and runaway slaves from the South, joined the Union army whenever they could. These "volunteers" cooked, tended the animals, dug trenches, hauled supplies, and helped in other ways. As the war continued, they were desperately needed. In July 1862 Congress allowed blacks to form fighting units as part of the army. Twenty-five thousand blacks also served in the Union navy.

From Louisiana to Massachusetts, free black regiments had begun organizing. In Missouri, in October 1862, ten black soldiers fell in battle, the first of their race to die in the Civil War. The governor of Massachusetts welcomed enough black soldiers to arm two regiments. One of these, the 54th Massachusetts, became the most famous unit of blacks in the war.

Cook, the Courageous Cannoneer

I worked as a cannoneer.

The Medal of Honor was established during the Civil War. Before then, no decorations were given to soldiers. It was thought that a soldier shouldn't get a medal for doing his duty. Senator James W. Grimes felt differently. On December 21, 1861, he introduced in Congress a bill to create a Medal of Honor to inspire soldiers to do their best. President Lincoln signed the bill, and the Medal of Honor was born. The Medal of Honor was given to those who acted bravely in battle.

John Cook wrote, "I was fifteen years of age, and was bugler of Battery B, which suffered fearful losses in the field at Antietam where I won my Medal of Honor.

"General Gibbon, our commander, had just ordered Lieutenant Stewart to take his section about one hundred yards to the right of the Hagerstown Pike, in front of two straw stacks. Lieutenant Stewart beckoned me to follow. No sooner had we unlimbered [readied the guns for action] when a column of Confederate infantry, emerging from the . . . west woods, poured a volley into us, which brought fourteen or seventeen of my brave comrades to the ground. The two straw stacks offered some shelter for our wounded, and it was a sickening sight to see those poor, maimed, and crippled fellows, crowding on top of one another, while several stepping but a few feet away, were hit again or killed.

"Just then Captain Campbell unlimbered the other four guns to the left of Stewart, and I reported to him. He had just dismounted, when he was hit twice, and his horse fell dead, with several bullets in its body. I started with the captain to the rear and turned him over to one of the [ambulance] drivers. He ordered me to report to Lieutenant Stewart and tell him to take command of the battery. I reported, and seeing the cannoneers nearly all down, one, with a pouch full of ammunition, lying dead, I unstrapped the pouch, started for the battery, and worked as a cannoneer. We were then in the vortex [center] of the battle. The enemy had made three desperate attempts to capture us, the last time coming within ten or fifteen feet of our guns. . . . At this battle we lost forty-four men, killed and wounded and about forty horses which shows how hard a fight it was."

John Cook received the Medal of Honor for his courage.

SHIRTS ON THE LINE

Dabney, a black cook and groom for the Union army, and his wife, a laundress for the rebels, helped the Union officers in a special way. Dabney knew the Virginia countryside well, and the Union generals welcomed his services. Often, he informed them of General Robert E. Lee's activities. He seemed to be right all the time, but the men were baffled by how he knew the enemy's every move.

Finally Dabney revealed his secret. He led the men to the riverbank. He pointed across to the Confederate side, where a cabin stood in the woods. Nearby, a clothesline stretched between two trees. Several colored flannel shirts hung on the line.

Dabney's wife, who cooked and washed laundry for Lee and his Confederate generals, had worked out a code. Each shirt stood for a specific officer. Mrs. Dabney listened to everything the generals planned. When an officer moved his troops, Mrs. Dabney went to the line and moved his shirt. If she took a shirt down, it meant the officer had ridden into Richmond. When she pinned two blankets together along the bottom, she was making a "fish-trap." The shape signaled to her husband that the enemy was plotting to trap the Yankees. The Confederates never discovered the married spy team.

WORDS OF COMFORT

The United States Sanitary Commission, which became the American Red Cross, was created during the Civil War. It helped set up hospitals and convalescent homes, buy medical supplies, and train nurses.

Doctors then knew little about germs. Diseases and infections spread quickly in the new hospitals.

Women organized more than 7,000 sanitary societies during the war. They volunteered to sew bandages and clothing for soldiers and to write letters to cheer them. One nurse wrote these words of comfort:

"My Dear Friend,

You are not my husband or son; but you are the husband or son of some woman who undoubtedly loves you as I love mine. I have made these garments for you with a heart that aches for your sufferings, and with a longing to come to you to assist in taking care of you. . . ."

U IS FOR UNIFORM

In the early months of the war, Union soldiers wore a variety of uniforms. New York soldiers wore their showy "Zouave" uniforms. Minnesota men wore red flannel shirts and black trousers. The Highland Scots of the 79th New York showed their ethnic pride by wearing kilted dress uniforms. As the war continued, all Yankee soldiers wore dark-blue blouses and light-blue pants, with a dark-blue caps, in the battlefield.

In the South, it was not uncommon for rebel soldiers to be without uniforms due to a shortage of clothing. Those lucky rebels who had uniforms mostly wore jackets of homespun wool and cotton. Natural "butternut" dyes were used to create a khaki-like color. They wore double-breasted light-gray blouses, sky-blue pants, and cloth caps. The cap's color was based on the soldier's branch of the service, such as infantry or cavalry.

Shoes were also in short supply in the Confederate army. The best place for rebel soldiers to find a pair of shoes was on the feet of a dead soldier. When shoes couldn't be found, rebel soldiers went barefoot.

Side by Side

Thomas J. Morgan, a white northern colonel in charge of four black regiments and the 14th U.S. Colored Infantry, described the end of a day's fighting. The battle took place at Nashville, Tennessee, in December 1864.

"General Steedman congratulated us, saying his only fear had been that we might fight too hard. We had done all he desired, and more. Colored soldiers had again fought side by side with white troops; they had mingled together in the charge; they had supported each other; they had assisted each other from the field when wounded, and they lay side by side in death. The survivors rejoiced together over a hard fought field."

"Calibre 54!"

"Send the cartridges right away!"

Eighteen-year-old Private George Henry Graffam served in the 30th Maine Infantry, Company B.

May 19, 1863, was another day of endless war at Vicksburg, Mississippi. Orion P. Howe, fourteen years old, was a drummer in the 55th Illinois. He and other musicians in his party were attached to a Union regiment commanded by Colonel Malmborg, located near the enemy barricade.

The regiment was dangerously low on ammunition. The colonel ordered the musicians to secure more bullets. Their destination was a quarter mile away, where the main body of Union troops was stationed.

The ground was covered with wood from shattered trees. The air was thick with bullets and smoke from rebel gun and cannon fire. Heavy shells hit the ground with such force that earth flew into the air and rained down upon the musicians.

Exposing himself to enemy shooters, Orion climbed the ridge. Suddenly he felt a searing pain in his leg. Orion was shot. He kept going, unaware that he was his regiment's last hope. All the other musicians had been killed by rebel fire.

Finally, Orion saw the road and the line of Union troops. Bleeding, he made his way to General Sherman and cried, "General Sherman, send some more cartridges to Colonel Malmborg; the men are all out."

"What is the matter, my boy?"

"They shot me in the leg, sir, but I can make it to the hospital. Send the cartridges right away!"

General Sherman told Orion to leave at once. He promised to attend to the cartridges. General Sherman watched Orion limp off. Just before he disappeared over the hill, Orion turned and called out loudly, "Calibre 54!"

Orion P. Howe was awarded the Medal of Honor for his bravery in battle.

THE UNSTOPPABLE GENERAL GRANT

In the autumn of 1862, General U. S. Grant and 40,000 men moved toward Vicksburg, a Mississippi city that stood on a bluff overlooking the river. It was one of the South's most important centers. If Grant could capture it, the South would be cut in two. For weeks, his men cut through forests and swamps to reach the city from the west. All the while, they were fired upon by rebels. After weeks of back-breaking work, they gave up.

Next, Grant attempted to reach the city from the east, by digging a canal that would bypass a wide bend in the river, where the Confederate army could fire down upon his men. With 40,000 shovels, the men began digging. But the river filled the canal with dirt and sand. When they tried dragging a gunboat through, the rebels shot at and destroyed the boat.

Grant would not give up. He and Admiral David Porter finally decided to sail their ironclad (iron-sided) ships and supply boats down the Mississippi River, right past the Confederates. The parade of Union ships included seven ironclads, several coal barges, three ships for carrying troops, and a ram. The people of Vicksburg watched in amazement.

With the wind in their favor, the Union fleet sailed fourteen miles down the river. Cannonballs flew and gunshots pelted them. The river glowed orange, but very few ships were destroyed.

After stopping a regiment of rebel soldiers that arrived with supplies for the starving people of Vicksburg, Grant's men surrounded the city. For forty-seven days, Grant's army and the Confederate soldiers fought desperately.

On June 15 Confederate General Johnston telegrammed his superior officer, "I consider saving Vicksburg hopeless." Starving residents ate whatever they could find. A hungry child said rat tasted like squirrel. The rebel army was weak and hungry.

On July 3 General Pemberton surrendered his 30,000 rebel troops with 60,000 rifles, 172 cannons, and tons of ammunition. General Grant would take no prisoners; he released the soldiers to go home and ordered treatment for all the wounded. He sent word of his victory to President Lincoln. Grant was later informed that on the same day, General Lee had surrendered at Gettysburg. The North had won the war's two most decisive battles. Northerners called it the best Fourth of July since 1776.

Thank You from the President

Before the battle at Vicksburg, Lincoln had told Grant that his strategy would not work. When it did, the president apologized to the general and put him in charge of all Union soldiers west of the Appalachian Mountains. Within a year, Grant was named general commander of the Union army. He had attained the highest possible military honor.

Rebel soldiers in Vicksburg shoot at Union iron-clad ships as they charge down the Mississippi River to assist General Grant. Before photography was invented, people depended on graphic art to show them current events such as boat races, parades, and even military battles. This chromolithograph was produced and sold by Nathaniel Currier and James Ives. Currier & Ives became famous for their graphic print business, which sold hand-colored, visually pleasing scenes of American life from the 1830s to 1904.

GETTYSBURG, THE BATTLE NO ONE PLANNED

It is spring 1863. Confederate General Robert E. Lee is worried about the reports he has received from Vicksburg, Mississippi. For months the Union army under General Grant has been attacking Vicksburg from one direction after another. The Confederates are holding fast, but Lee knows they are in trouble. Somehow, he must lure Grant away from the Mississippi River.

By June, Lee had a plan. He would lead his Army of Northern Virginia to Harrisburg, Pennsylvania, and fight on Yankee soil. A victory would give his troops supplies they desperately needed. Lee hoped Grant would come after him. Lee's 75,000 men and artillery moved north. When they reached Gettysburg, Pennsylvania, Lee sent some soldiers into town to find shoes for his men.

There, on July first, they were surprised to meet Union soldiers who also happened to be on the road to town. Without orders, the armies opened fire. Defeated by the Confederates, the Union sol-

Baking Bread for the Union

Jenny Wade, a teenager, was making bread in her family home near the Gettysburg battlefield. She paid no attention to the sound of rebel and Yankee gunfire, nor to pleas from soldiers to leave. Her only concern was feeding the Union troops.

Jenny Wade's efforts were stopped by a stray bullet from the gunfire surrounding her home. The bullet entered her heart and killed her. Her body was placed in an abandoned enemy coffin. She was buried in Gettysburg.

diers scattered. Lee hadn't intended to fight at Gettysburg; now he would not back down.

The retreating Union soldiers climbed into the hilly countryside south of town. Their commander, General George Meade, ordered the rest of his 88,000 men of the Army of the Potomac to follow. They moved up into the hills and along Cemetery Ridge, southeast of town, covering an area of nearly three miles.

The next morning, Lee's army attacked. All day, smoke clouded the sky. Gunshots, shouts, and the moans of the injured pierced the air. Soldiers fell groaning into pools of blood as comrades took their places. The armies fought late into the night. But the Confederates could not drive the Union army from the hills.

On July 3, Lee assembled every soldier he had. His men were reinforced by the 15,000-man army of General George Pickett. The North was protected by trees behind them; the South approached with every cannon and rifle it had. For two hours the armies exchanged fire. When the artillery fire died down, Lee's army made its unforgettable appearance.

It marched in a perfect unit, one mile wide. Flags flew at the middle, with officers on horseback. Rifles gleamed in the sun. The wall of soldiers advanced through the woods, across the field, and up the ridge. It looked like a human fortress. But it wasn't.

The Union soldiers watched them advance. "We could not help hitting them at every shot," a Union officer said later. As the rebel army approached, a Union general on horseback rode along the line, with instructions: "Do not hurry . . . let them come up close before you fire and then aim slow."

By the time the armies clashed on the ridge, 10,000 Confederates had already fallen. Those who remained were badly outnumbered. "Men fire into each other's faces, not five feet apart," a soldier later wrote. "There are ghastly heaps of dead men." Only half of the rebels who marched out returned. On July 4 the Confederates dragged themselves through the pounding rain and escaped across the Potomac River onto Confederate soil. The battle of Gettysburg had crippled the South.

After the battle, the people of Gettysburg set up hospital tents to care for tens of thousands of wounded Yankees and to bury the 8,000 who had died; 50,000 men were killed, missing, or wounded. President Lincoln hoped that with General Meade's victory, the "rebellion must dwindle and die." But for nearly two more years, the war dragged on.

I'm Here to Fight!

The flag fell to the ground.

Nathaniel Gwynne knew he was too young to enlist in the Union army. That didn't stop him. He pestered Union officers until a captain of Company H, 13th Ohio Calvary, agreed to let him come along. He could perform all the duties of a private—except going into battle.

But on July 30, 1864, in Petersburg, Virginia, Nathaniel disobeyed his captain. When the men lined up to charge the rebels on Fort Hill, Nathaniel lined up with them. The captain reminded him he wasn't enlisted and told him to stay behind.

Nathaniel said, "But that's not what I'm here for!"

When the bugle sounded, he joined the Union calvary in battle. The rebels quickly overwhelmed the Union forces. They drove the Union troops back, and captured the Union flag.

Nathaniel jumped on a horse and rode into the rebel fire, determined to recapture the cavalry's flag. Dodging bullets and shells, he reached the enemy line and brazenly reclaimed the flag. Now he had to get back.

Holding the colors in one hand, Nathaniel focused his attention on reaching the cavalry. The rebels focused their attention and guns on Nathaniel. A shell hit Nathaniel's arm carrying the flag. His arm was shattered by the blast. The flag fell to the ground. He stopped, picked up the flag with his good arm, took the reins of his horse in his teeth, and continued. A bullet pierced Nathaniel's leg. He continued on.

When Nathaniel finally reached his troops, he handed his comrades the flag and fell off his horse, unconscious. That very day Nathaniel was enlisted into the Ohio Cavalry and later received the Medal of Honor for his act of bravery.

Make a Dog Tent

In order to defeat the South, Union troops constantly needed to move from somewhere in the North to somewhere in the South.

Montgomery Meigs, who was in charge of supplying the Union army, realized that having lighter equipment would make the army more mobile. He substituted the heavy tents used previously with lighter ones called "dog tents" by northern troops. Today these tents are known as "pup tents."

You can make your own pup tent. Here's how.

You Will Need:

One blanket or sheet; rope (the length is dependent on the distance between the trees, posts, or chairs); two trees, posts, or chairs (if you're doing this indoors); and rocks or weighted objects (at least four). Optional: a blanket or rug can be used as a tent floor.

1. Find two trees and/or posts with open space between them. If you're doing this indoors, place two chairs about six feet apart.

2. Tie each end of the rope around the trees, posts, or chairs. Make sure the rope is tied tightly!

3. Drape your blanket or sheet over the rope.

4. Place a rock or weighted object on each corner of your tent.

Your pup tent is ready! Why not make a Civil War evening of it? Invite some friends over. Dress up in Confederate or Union uniforms. Make a recipe from this book. For entertainment, play marbles or take turns reading from or playing a game in this book.

THE RELUCTANT SPY

David O. Dodd never wanted to be a spy. But he was back in his hometown of Little Rock, Arkansas, on trial for being a Confederate agent.

He had traveled from Monroe, Louisiana, to Little Rock on family business. His older brother was confident that David's young age would make it easier for him to travel from Confederate Louisiana into Union-held Arkansas.

To go to Little Rock, Dodd needed the Confederate army's permission. The local commander was willing to give Dodd a travel pass, but only if he agreed to gather information about Union forces.

Dodd arrived in Little Rock just before Christmas. During his visit, he stayed with his aunt, socialized with girls, and went to dances. He also gathered facts about Union forces with the help of a friend.

Dodd tried to think like a spy. He knew it would be foolish to record what he had learned in plain English. Anyone who got a look at his notebook would instantly know what he was up to. Dodd decided to enter the information in his notebook in Morse code. Unfortunately, Morse code was not only the language of the telegraph; it was also the most obvious language of a spy.

On December 29 David Dodd decided to return to Monroe, Louisiana. With his notebook and a Union pass among his possessions, Dodd started out of town on a mule, satisfied he had been a good brother and conscientious spy.

Up ahead stood a Union sentry. Dodd wasn't concerned; he had a travel pass. The sentry let Dodd ride on. The second sentry stopped Dodd and asked where he was going. Dodd falsely replied he was going about fifteen miles into the country. The sentry asked for Dodd's pass and kept it. A pass wasn't needed for short journeys. Dodd didn't protest. The sentry was simply following procedure.

The third sentry, Lieutenant Stopral, asked Dodd for his pass. Dodd told him that another sentry had taken it. Stopral became suspicious and arrested him.

Dodd was searched. Lieutenant Stopral found Louisiana money, a Confederate pass and postage stamps, a loaded Derringer pistol, letters, and the notebook with Morse code records. Dodd was tried as a spy. On January 5, 1864, he was convicted and sentenced to death.

Dodd wrote to President Lincoln and Congress hoping they would reverse his sentence. "I ask you therefore to look with charity on the circumstances which surround an unfortunate youth, living at a time in an age and a country filled with commotions, so extraordinary, as to deceive and ensnare many patriotic citizens in all parts of the Republic! Will [you] reflect, O my judges, that I have just entered upon the threshold of life.... Will you consider that my school books daily call to mind the deeds of Washington, the achievement of our common ancestors, and the greatness of that flag which protects us all: and that if one sentiment in my youthful breast predominates over another, it is that which gives us a common fame and a common glory."

David Dodd was executed on January 8, 1864.

DECIPHER A SPY'S JOURNAL

Pictured at right is a page from David Dodd's notebook. It is written in Morse code. Can you discover what he wrote down about the Union forces? Use the Morse code alphabet provided here to decipher Dodd's code.

A	._	M	__	Y	_.__
B	_...	N	_.	Z	__..
C	_._.	O	___	1	.____
D	_..	P	.__.	2	..___
E	.	Q	__._	3	...__
F	.._.	R	._.	4	...._
G	__.	S	...	5	.....
H	....	T	_	6	_....
I	..	U	.._	7	__...
J	.___	V	..._	8	___..
K	_._	W	.__	9	____.
L	._..	X	_.._	0	_____

Are you finding misspelled or nonsense words? Well, so did we. And so did Lieutenant Stopral, who deciphered this page more than 130 years ago.

David Dodd didn't remember the entire Morse code. When he couldn't remember what a letter was in Morse code, he used a number, letter, or drawings instead. Also, his spacing between dots and dashes wasn't perfect. Lieutenant Stopral surely realized this and, most likely, tried matching odd words with common military items. For example "bsass" meant brass, as in brass gun.

Now that you know this, try again. This time be aware that Dodd was unsure of the Morse code for the letters *o, r,* and *y.* Also, all his information was about two Ohio batteries. If you're still stumped, you'll find a translation on page 92.

Dear Uncle

This is my first letter, so you must excuse all mistakes. I have never gone to school yet, but ma says she will send me to school, when the war over, all the little girls here goes to school I would like to go so much, but I do not let them get ahead of me, Lily says he will write the next time all join one in love to you

your Dear niece Cora

Make Your Own Code

Morse code, the language of the telegraph, was an important means of communication during the Civil War. It was also a spy code. A more subtle code used ordinary words that had hidden meanings. A spy placed these words in a certain order among the words of a letter or note. The trick was to have the letter make sense.

Can you do it? Create a collection of ordinary words that have special meanings to you and a friend. Choose one person to write a letter, including some or all of these special words. Have another pair of friends follow the same procedure. Intercept each other's letters. Who can figure out the intercepted message first?

U.S. FLAG STEAMER "PHILADELPHIA" MAY 23d 1864

MY DEAR BROTHERS,

YOUR NICE LETTER SHOULD HAVE BEEN ANSWERED LONG AGO FOR IT WAS VERY NICELY DONE AND I AM GLAD TO SEE HOW YOU HAVE IMPROVED. BY AND BYE I SHALL EXPECT ONE WRITTEN LIKE SISTER MARIA'S.

A SHIP'S BOAT

WHILE "BRUZ" WAS DOWN IN THE ST JOHN'S RIVER, THE OLD REBELS USED TO PUT TORPEDOES IN THE RIVER AND OUR BIG STEAMBOAT WOULD RUN AGAINST THEM & THEN BLOW UP. HERE IS A PICTURE OF THE ONE BRUZ TOOK.

IT WAS FULL OF POWDER 80 POUNDS

THE STEAMER WOULD HIT THE THINGS YOU SEE STICKING UP & THAT WOULD LIGHT THE POWDER AND UP MR. STEAMER WOULD GO AND THEN SINK.

HERE ARE TWO THAT WERE BLOWN UP NEAR THE SAME PLACE

MAPLE LEAF   GEN'L HUNTER

WASN'T IT MEAN OF THE REBELS TO BLOW PEOPLE UP WHILE THEY WERE ASLEEP?

GIVE MY LOVE TO ALL AND WRITE ME ANOTHER LETTER

YOUR AFFECTIONATE BRO'
JOHN.

TO MASTERS
BILL & BOB
PEGRAM

MY DEAR LITTLE SON

During the Civil War, the letter was the most frequent form of communication. To hold a letter in battle from a father or brother was to hold him. To hear his words was to see him. For a soldier in the battlefield, to read and reread letters from home was to escape the pain of battle, for a moment, and delight in the illusion of being home. On this page and the preceding one are four Civil War letters.

At right, George Loyal Gordon is writing home to his son Armistead Churchill Gordon. Below is the son's reply. George Gordon was in the 5th North Carolina Regiment. He died July 1, 1862, during a battle at Malvern Hill.

Opposite, far left: This letter was written by young Cora to her uncle, date unknown.
Left: This letter was written by John Pegram to his brothers from the ship *Philadelphia.*

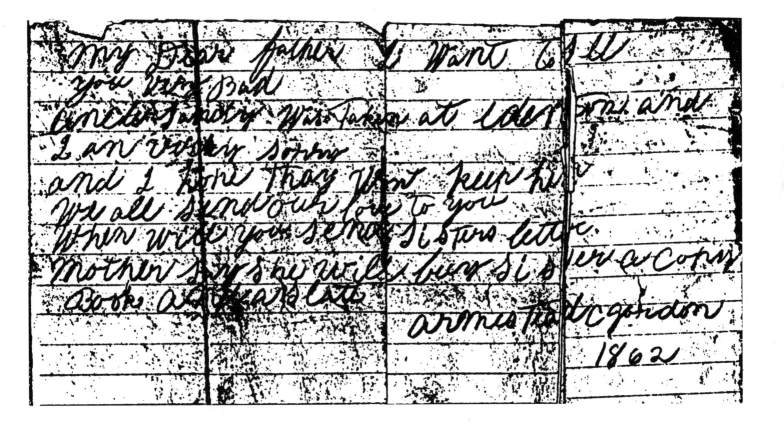

One was knitting a pair of socks.

A BOX FOR THE SOLDIER

Though small children couldn't go to war, they sent boxes of clothing and goodies to fathers and brothers who were in battle. In *The Student and Schoolmate* of March 1864, Mrs. Phebe H. Phelps wrote an article "A Box for the Soldier." The following are excerpts.

"One of the daughters was knitting a pair of socks, soft and thick, for the weary feet that must stand all day in the cold, wet trenches. . . .

"The youngest daughter only five years old, the darling . . . was trying her little unskillful fingers on a cap [making a cap] for papa. . . . 'Ah,' she kept saying, "poor dear papa! how I would like to have papa's head close to mine, on my little pillow! I don't like to have him sleep on the bare ground!'

"What *could* boys put in? What could they make? One of them put in his knife,—the knife he prized so much,—all the knife he had, for he thought father might have lost his and would want one. . . .

"'I'm sure,' said one of the knitters, 'that father will like my socks the best of anything, for there's nothing so bad as cold feet.' . . .

"'Why we never thought of the things that mother is going to send! Of course, father will like them best,' exclaimed one of the children. 'She sends so many nice things; flannels and other clothes, and jellies, and cakes, and everything she can think of. And then I saw her writing such a long letter, with the tears on her cheeks! I know it's a beautiful letter, and I know father'll like that letter better than everything in the box. You see if he don't.'"

DYING INCH BY INCH

Many Yankee and rebel soldiers died from enemy fire. Some were hanged as spies. Many more died from disease. Others, however, died as prisoners of war. For captured rebels, the worst camp was in Elmira, New York. For captured Yankees, the worst camp was in Andersonville, Georgia.

In Andersonville, by 1864, 33,000 Yankees, black and white, lived in a camp intended for 10,000 prisoners. Men lived in shabby shelters that did little to protect them from winter's cold or summer's heat. During one summer day, 300 sick and wounded died.

In their diaries, prisoners cried out for help: "What can the government be thinking of to let soldiers die in this filthy place?" "Can a government exist and let their men die inch by inch here?"

"Embalming bodies has become quite a business at Washington. One physician is said to have made $50,000. The prices are $50 for an officer, and $25 for a private." (*The School and Schoolmate*, August 1862)

THE BATTLE FOR RICHMOND

By April 2, 1865, it was certain. Yankee forces were about to storm the Confederate capital. General Grant and the Union forces had broken through General Robert E. Lee's Confederate line. Enemy guns flashed in the near distance.

At 5 A.M., on April 3, Richmond was shaken by a violent explosion. Lucy Fletcher, like other residents in the city, could only watch in horror. In her diary she wrote, "A tremendous explosion shook the whole city and we knew that our fate was sealed." Confederate troops had set gunboats and gunpowder magazines on fire so Union troops wouldn't get them. The fire spread quickly.

Lucy Fletcher wrote, "The atmosphere was lurid with flame and smoke of the burning buildings while the constant explosion of loaded shells and other combustibles scattered the burning brands in every direction and filled the air with deadly missiles which raked the streets and went crashing through the windows."

From this madness Southerners had fled the city, including President Jefferson Davis and his family. Into the city came Yankee victors, including regiments of black cavalry and infantry soldiers.

Forty hours later, President Abraham Lincoln himself sat in the Confederate White House. Lincoln's arrival in Richmond drew a large crowd of ecstatic black people overwhelmed by the sight of the man who had set them free.

There were shouts of "Glory to God!" One woman shouted, "I know I am free for I have seen Father Abraham and felt him." One black man fell on his knees before Lincoln. Lincoln said, "Don't kneel to me. That is not right. You must kneel to God only, and thank Him for the liberty you will enjoy hereafter."

Much of Richmond, Virginia, lay in ruins after the Yankee attack, which began on April 3, 1865.

Surrender at Appomattox

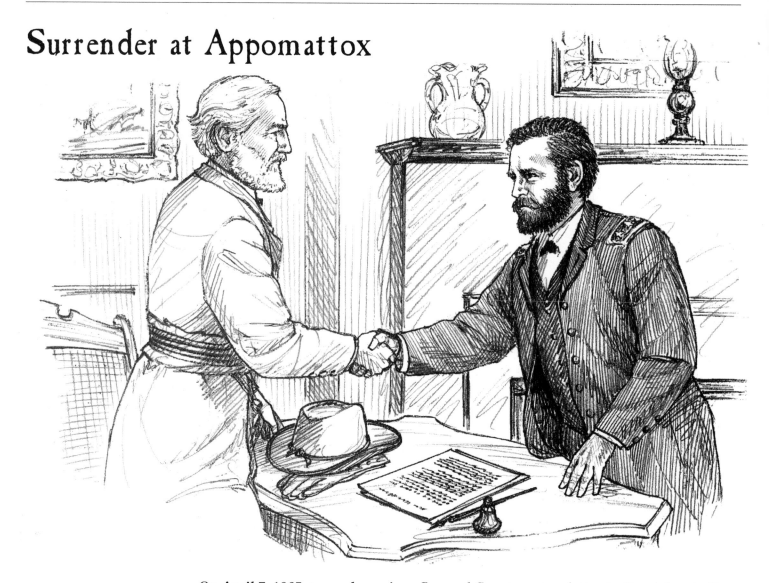

Ulysses S. Grant

On April 7, 1865, toward evening, General Grant wrote a letter to Confederate General Robert E. Lee. He knew that Lee's troops were hungry and too weak to defend themselves. It was senseless to continue fighting. In part, he wrote, "I . . . [am] asking . . . you [to] surrender . . . that portion of the Confederate States army known as the Army of Northern Virginia."

That same evening, General Lee and his men camped nearby in some woods. They were muddy, their eyes dull with exhaustion and defeat. They sat on blankets spread on the ground. They had built a fire. They had no chairs, no stools, no tent, no table, no food, no reserve troops. The Union army outnumbered them at least four to one.

In the morning, Lee faced the reality. He could do nothing but surrender. He sent a foot soldier to carry a white towel, a signal of surrender, and a note to Grant. He would like to meet. As he waited for the answer, he selected a trim brick house in the village for the occasion.

On April 9, soldiers sprawled on the springtime farmland grass while the officers met in the parlor, sitting at separate tables. Wilmer McLean, owner of the house, had granted them his permission. Robert E. Lee, white-haired and bearded, arrived at the house first. Trim and elegant, he wore a spotless new uniform. His jeweled dress sword hung at his side, and his high black riding boots were polished. He explained that he had expected to be taken prisoner.

When Grant arrived, he greeted Lee warmly and offered his hand. Grant, a man of rough, natural dignity, was far from camp and his dress uniform. To spare Lee further delay, he had borrowed a private's jacket. His shirt was wrinkled, and mud covered his boots. He rarely rode with his sword and didn't have it now. He talked pleasantly of meeting General Lee in the Mexican War, many years earlier. Both had graduated from the military academy at West Point, but Lee was older by a dozen years.

Robert E. Lee

The two generals met for nearly two hours, while Grant wrote out the terms he had already thought about. Lincoln had also advised him. "Give them horses to plow with, and guns to shoot crows. I want no one punished," the president had declared.

Grant told Lee that when rebel weapons and government property were returned to the Union army, Lee's men could go home. There would be no trials, no prisoners. Lee asked that the men be allowed to keep their horses. "Yes," the general replied. Lee's men were also hungry. Could rations be found? "Yes," again came Grant's reply. When Union soldiers began firing cannons to celebrate their victory, Grant stopped them. "The rebels are our countrymen again," he said. The best sign of rejoicing would be "to abstain from all demonstrations."

"With malice toward none; with charity toward all," Abraham Lincoln had said just a month earlier at his second inauguration. The "horrid dream" the president had lived during four years of the Civil War was ending.

Three days after the agreement was signed, the Army of Northern Virginia marched past Union troops, placing their weapons and battle flags in a great pile. In the hush, as the bugles blew "Cease Fire," the soldiers wept.

"We Are All Americans"

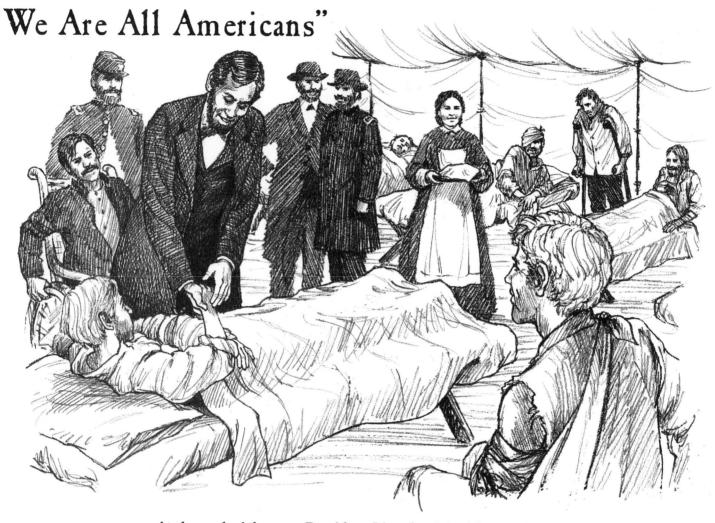

At the end of the war, President Lincoln visited hospital tents that held wounded soldiers. He walked among the rows, shaking hands. When he came to cots where rebel soldiers lay, he shook their hands, too. One southern soldier stopped him and asked, "Do you know who I am?" President Lincoln said no.

"I am a Confederate colonel who has fought you as hard as he could for four years," the soldier told him.

"Well," said Lincoln, "I hope a Confederate colonel will not refuse me his hand."

"No, sir," the officer replied, "I will not." The two men shook hands, and Lincoln moved to the next cot.

Others also tried to heal the scars of war. When General Grant drew up the surrender agreement for General Lee to sign, he acted with dignity and kindness. Grant chose the words, but his assistant, Colonel Ely Parker, wrote the copies to be signed.

Ely S. Parker was a full-blooded Seneca Indian, an engineer by trade, and a leader among American Indians. During the war, Grant made Parker his secretary. Parker was always at the general's side. He carried the general's "briefcase" and a supply of paper and ink.

According to witnesses at Appomattox, General Lee was surprised to see Parker among the officers with Grant. When Lee and Parker were introduced, Lee studied the Indian's brown skin, broad cheekbones, and straight dark hair. Seconds later, he spoke. "I am glad to see one real American here."

Colonel Parker's reply was brief: "We are *all* Americans," he told the general.

THE NATION MOURNS

On Sunday, April 9, 1865, General Robert E. Lee signed the surrender agreement. Some southern officers would still try to resupply their soldiers and continue fighting. But the Civil War was over.

In Washington two nights later, Lincoln stood outside on the upper balcony of the White House and spoke to the crowd gathered on the lawn below. He spoke of the hard work that lay ahead as the nation rebuilt. He wanted the nation's wounds to heal, forgiveness to begin, and the Union to grow strong once more.

For Lincoln, the end of the war brought huge relief. His patience and wisdom had helped preserve the nation. As he thought about the end of his second term in office, he looked forward to returning to his law practice in Illinois. He and Mary might travel.

On Friday evening of that week, the Lincolns went to the theater. The audience applauded as the couple made their way into the presidential box. An hour into the entertainment, a single gunshot rang out. Lincoln slumped forward. He was rushed to a house across the street from the theater, but he could not be saved. President Lincoln died on Saturday morning, April 15, 1865.

As Andrew Johnson took the oath of office, Lincoln's funeral was planned. After a small service in the White House, his body lay in state in the Capitol for two days, so Americans could honor his life. His casket was placed aboard a funeral train. His portrait was displayed on the engine as it slowly made its way to Illinois. Newspapers announced that Lincoln's killer, John Booth, had been trapped by federal agents. He, too, was dead.

Seven million people stood in silence as they watched the dark train roll past. Never before had a president been assassinated. Americans were stunned and stricken with grief. The president was buried in Springfield, Illinois. Northerners and many Southerners alike worried about what his death would mean. For blacks, the voice of their greatest advocate had been silenced.

In time, joy would replace sorrow as Americans remembered Abraham Lincoln, not as the great man who had been taken from them but as the one who had been given to them briefly, when he was needed most.

President Lincoln and his son Tad strolled through Richmond, Virginia, the fallen Confederate capital, in April 1865. Free slaves cheered as the two walked by.

A Family Reunited

Archibald Henry Grimké finished his speech and sat down. He had addressed his fellow students at Lincoln University. The year was 1868. Archibald and his brother Francis were both second-year students at the school for black men. They both had been born in Charleston, South Carolina. Their church back home was paying their tuition, but the boys had very little money to live on.

A few days later, Archie received a letter in the mail. He did not recognize the handwriting. Tearing the envelope open, he read the sender's name. Angelina Grimké Weld. She wrote to ask if he might be the former slave of her brother, Dr. John Grimké, of Charleston. She closed her letter by describing her anti-slavery activities.

Archie wrote back immediately. Into the letter he tucked two pictures. He told her that he was the son of her other brother, Henry. Archie was three when his father died, in 1853. He and his two baby brothers were given to their father's white son, Montague. Montague let them live with their mother until he married. But then he wanted them for his servants. Archie ran away.

Angelina and her sister Sarah read this letter. Their unusual last name had led them to think that Archibald might be their relative. As they looked at the photographs, they could not doubt that he was their brother's child. Suddenly the work the sisters had done all their lives, helping the cause of black freedom, had a different meaning. They had been working for the children of their own family.

Aunt Sarah was delighted to find her nephews. At seventy-six, Sarah was old. But her nephews brought their youth and love into her life. As the two generations of Grimkés got to know each other, the boys came often to spend time at their aunts' home.

When Archibald and Francis graduated from Lincoln University in 1870, Sarah, Angelina, and Theodore Weld were there to watch. Next the young men chose graduate schools and found work to earn money while they studied. To Sarah their lives were a new adventure. In a way they were like the children she had never had.

Sarah wanted to help them. She had very little money, but that didn't stop her. She wrote a novel about a racially mixed family, hoping to make some money for her "Archie-fund," as she called it.

In 1874 Archibald graduated from Harvard Law School. He became a writer and activist for the black cause. He traveled to Santo Domingo as United States consul and held an officer's post in the National Association for the Advancement of Colored People (NAACP), a powerful national organization.

Aunt Sarah did not live to see all this. She died in 1873, not long before Archie's graduation from Harvard. But her gift to her heirs lived on. Archie, an outstanding black leader in the late nineteenth century and into the twentieth, received the NAACP's highest honor, the Spingarn Medal, for achievement by an American citizen of African descent.

Archie found his aunts' lives an inspiration and a big influence on his own. He told others that they made him "a liberal in religion, a radical in the woman's suffrage movement, in politics, and on the race question." He and his wife, Sarah Stanley, named their daughter Angelina Weld Grimké.

What Happened to Francis Grimké?

When the Civil War began, Francis Grimké ran away from his master and half-brother. He joined the Confederate army as an officer's valet, or personal servant.

When the war ended, he was sent north to be educated. He was helped by a woman in Charleston, whose church found enough money to send him and his brother Archie to college.

Francis graduated from Lincoln University. With his aunts' help, he went on to study for the ministry. Until his death, he served as a Presbyterian minister and for many years was an officer of Howard University.

M IS FOR ME

Me? Now you know some things about the Civil War. But what does the Civil War have to do with *you*? This letter is unique, because you are the only one who can answer the question. If you're African-American, the war was about your ancestors' rights. Perhaps someone in your family fought in the war. Depending on where you live, battles may have been fought in your backyard. Has your family kept Civil War rifles or sabers that your great-great-grandfather or someone else used? Find out. Ask your parents if and how the war affected your family in some way.

If You Want to Know More

The book must stop, but you don't have to. There is so much more to explore in the American Civil War. This section lists books to read, internet websites, activities to try, and trips that will help you increase your understanding of the time when Americans went to war against Americans.

Books

Books, books, there are so many books on the American Civil War. Your librarian can offer you many rewarding options to expand your knowledge and further pique your interest. Here are several books to get you started:

Women were participants not observers during the American Civil War. They nursed wounded soldiers. Women disguised themselves as men so they could fight. They were single parents raising their children. Read *A Separate Battle: Women and the Civil War*, by Ina Chang (New York: Scholastic, 1991), to gain a richer understanding of the accomplishments of women during the American Civil War.

The war was over. Black Americans wanted the same opportunity for success granted to any white American. They didn't get it. Many black Americans joined the U.S. cavalry, hoping to achieve success. Read *The Forgotten Heroes: The Story of the Buffalo Soldiers*, by Clinton Cox (New York: Scholastic, 1993), to learn how the black American struggle for equality after the Civil War was anything but easy.

Baseball and the Civil War. Contests. Fascinating facts. It's all in *The Children's Chronicle: A Civil War Newsletter*, a wonderful children's newsletter compiled by George McNamara. If you want to purchase back issues or sign up for coming issues, write to: George McNamara, P.O. Box 6393, Philadelphia, PA 19136.

The Civil War on the Net

Check out the internet at your local library or on your personal computer. The net is a wonderful source for Civil War information, pictures, and events. Here are some examples:

Want to explore the Morse code further? There's a great website called "Morse Code Translator." Its address is: http://www.soton.ac.uk/scp93ch/refer/morseform.html. This site will translate your typed statements in Morse code, then play it back to you so you can hear the dots and dashes.

Interested in Civil War pictures? Check out this Library of Congress website: http://rs6.loc.gov/cwphome.html. Also check out the Civil War Homepage at: http://funnelweb.utcc.utk.edu/%7Ehoemann/warweb.html.

Every year dozens of men and women, boys and girls, gather to reenact various Civil War battles. For more information, check out this website address: http://www.fastlane.net/homepages/petro/reenact.html. For information about African-American Civil War reenactments, contact Q.M. Sargent George Hughes, 803-795-8438.

Trips

You've read this book; now visit one of our nation's Civil War National Parks. The Manassas National Battlefield Park, in Manassas, Virginia, should be on your list. This park has numerous programs that offer visitors an opportunity to see how Civil War soldiers drilled, fired weapons, and developed battlefield strategy. For more information, call 703-361-1339.

If you're headed to Boston, check out the Robert Gould Shaw and 54th Regiment Memorial. For more information, write The Museum of Afro-American History, 46 Joy Street, Boston, MA 02114. Headed to Washington, D.C.? Visit the African-American Civil War Memorial that was dedicated in 1996.

Answer to Morse code message on page 79: *3rd Ohio battery has 4 guns brass. 11th Ohio battery* [handwritten "B" on page stands for battery] *has 6 guns brass.*

Index

Acknowledgments

Acknowledgment is given to the following institutions and individuals for permission to reprint the photographs, letters, broadsides, and artworks that appear in this book:

PAGE 11
top, The Museum of the Confederacy, Richmond, Virginia; *bottom*, Yale University Art Gallery, New Haven, Connecticut.

PAGE 38
Library of Congress, Washington, D.C.

PAGE 39
top, California State Library, Sacramento, California; *bottom*, private collection of Richard Orsi.

PAGE 41
top, private collection of Richard Orsi; *bottom*, private collection of Richard Orsi.

PAGE 42
Library of Congress, Washington, D.C.

PAGE 43
top, U.S. Army Military History Institute, Carlisle, Pennsylvania; *bottom*, private collection of James J. Rawls.

PAGE 47
Corbis-Bettmann Archive, New York, New York.

PAGE 50
Lincoln National Life Foundation, Fort Wayne, Indiana.

PAGE 52
Library of Congress, Washington, D.C.

PAGE 55
Library of Congress, Washington, D.C.

PAGE 56
far left, National Archives, Washington, D.C., and The Museum of the Confederacy, Richmond, Virginia; *left*, private collection of Robert J. Chandler.

PAGE 65
National Archives, Washington, D.C.

PAGE 66
Library of Congress, Washington, D.C.

PAGE 67
top left, Hargrett Rare Book and Manuscript Library, University of Georgia, Athens, Georgia; *all other photographs*, Library of Congress, Washington, D.C.

PAGE 68
Library of Congress, Washington, D.C., and The Museum of the Confederacy, Richmond, Virginia.

PAGE 69
Library of Congress, Washington, D.C.

PAGE 70
National Archives, Washington, D.C.

PAGE 71
Library of Congress, Washington, D.C.

PAGE 72
The Congressional Medal of Honor Society, Mt. Pleasant, South Carolina.

PAGE 74
Library of Congress, Washington, D.C.

PAGE 75
U.S. Naval Academy Museum, Annapolis, Maryland.

PAGE 76
Library of Congress, Washington, D.C.

PAGE 80
left, The Museum of the Confederacy, Richmond, Virginia; *right*, The Library of the University of North Carolina, Chapel Hill, North Carolina.

PAGE 81
Virginia Historical Society, Richmond, Virginia.

PAGE 82
Library of Congress, Washington, D.C.

PAGE 83
Library of Congress, Washington, D.C.

PAGE 84
The National Portrait Gallery, Washington, D.C.

PAGE 85
The National Portrait Gallery, Washington, D.C.

PAGE 87
bottom, National Portrait Gallery, Washington, D.C.